POETRY
WALES
forty years

EDITED BY ROBERT MINHINNICK

POETRY WALES
forty years

seren

Seren is the book imprint of
Poetry Wales Press Ltd
Nolton Street, Bridgend, Wales
www.seren-books.com

Introduction & Editorial © Robert Minhinnick, 2005

ISBN 1-85411-379-8

The publisher works with the financial assistance
of the Welsh Books Council.

Cover painting: Harry Hong – Acrylic on perspex by Elfyn Lewis.
www.elfynlewis.com

Printed by CPD, Ebbw Vale

Contents

Introduction

The Pocket Anglo-Welsh Canon

One day, you and I will walk the aisles of libraries,
with their plausible stink of the shut generations,
to pass over an entire canon that's long been thumbed
to stub and take from some or other imagined shelf
the intimate apocrypha.
                         Cloth binding
will be opened-out in prayer, the warp of weather
down the stone and across denominations, where air
is more than lost, gone a pointillism of coal dust. I mean
the cant of the great and good who never made us famous,
and in the first language, namely *English*. And I swear
that though these words were never ours,
they will have happened like a history, share that taste
of copper on the tongue, have a certain easiness
with human heat; they'll be the pure that's cast
by men in ballots, a pickling of steel.
How the negative was to right the light from dark,
the schoolroom's slag-flood glare will wake dead arms.
This, the book we hold and in our hands.

KATHRYN GRAY

COMPILING *POETRY WALES – 25 YEARS* (Seren, 1990), Cary Archard wrote "…making this anthology has been an almost impossible task. The final selection is bound to seem somewhat arbitrary when the editor is forced to reduce some 10,000 items from 94 separate issues to one book".

Poetry Wales – 40 Years is compiled from 154 issues of the magazine. As a principle, nothing included in Cary Archard's anthology is used here. But if the selection seems arbitrary it is not intended as such. What we have is an anthology of Welsh writing in English from 1965 until 2005. It contains some brilliant and contentious work presented in what I see as a conservative and coherent collection. (Although personally I believe incoherence has something to be said for it.)

Because of the varieties of material available it would have been possible to produce an *anti-Poetry Wales – 40 Years* that contained not a word about the host country yet was a tribute to its expansiveness. Some readers might see that as a missed opportunity. Instead, what have been sacrificed are most of the magazine's international interests and almost all of the poets who publish from outside Wales, or indeed in Welsh.

All my adult life I have been in some ways involved with *Poetry Wales*. It's hard to over-emphasise the excitement of the initial encounter of a writer with the magazine that publishes his first work. For me it was *PW* Volume 8:2. Then *Poetry Wales* seemed lean, beautiful, authoritative. For someone like myself, working outside academia and unconnected to the literary world, the magazine was a miracle. Viewing it in Cardiff bookshops, or upon its three monthly arrival at home in the mid 1970s, was an extraordinary thrill. Despite the medieval seals and ancient lettering its covers carried, *Poetry Wales* felt modern. Other Welsh magazines were more puzzling. *The Anglo-Welsh Review* was a vast and fusty wardrobe. *Planet* seemed not to comprehend the English-speaking Wales I inhabited.

By the time I started reading *Poetry Wales* (from 1972) its nationalist heyday was over. There remained anger, idealism and sometimes vilification but the magazine had changed. Founder Meic Stephens's own poetry stopped dead in its tracks, while John Tripp, for all his ferocity, is best remembered for biographical pieces on other writers and a vision of a world of plenty glimpsed through hotel windows. Harri Webb had already written his best work. Indeed, in 1971, his 'That Summer' was rejected by the then editor. This appalled Webb. "When *PW* refused to print it", he has written, "I lost interest in the magazine". That's not quite true, as he continued to publish occasionally, but it's an indication of the problems facing any magazine with entrenched contributors.

It was left to Roland Mathias, Raymond Garlick and Tony Conran to use the magazine as a means of developing their philosophical ideas of Wales as a culturally-nurturing, politically radical and independent entity. But all three writers' visions were private and idealised and their work still awaits proper appreciation. As for R.S. Thomas, two special issues (7:4 & 29:1) were devoted to his life and writing, but neither his important religious poetry nor his most notoriously vitriolic comments on English-speaking Wales appeared in the magazine. Scholarship, integral from the outset, had ensured special numbers on such writers as Dafydd ap Gwilym, David Jones and Edward Thomas. As to translation, most of it came from the Welsh, with the American, Joseph Clancy, establishing a fruitful relationship with the magazine. But readers will note only a small amount of translation in this anthology. What the four decades of *Poetry Wales* reveal is a failure of literary interaction between the country's languages. (By this I mean creative translation from the Welsh.) One reason for this is that the approach of most English language poets to Welsh has been paralysed by deference.

As to the editors, none of them after the 1960s used the magazine to pursue a manifest agenda, although Mike Jenkins's green community socialism caught the political flavour of the 1980s – at least for those alienated by the politics of Margaret Thatcher. As for 'political' poetry, we can now judge that this had been well written by a tiny handful of people, and its day was done before the editorships of Sam Adams, John Powell Ward, Cary Archard and Richard Poole, which all concentrated on introducing new writers and promoting the deserving. Even Mike Jenkins could not discover any worthwhile overtly political verse, although his 'Red Poets' Society' still strives to do this. Regarding 'special numbers', if there was to be one from the late 1970s on, it would as likely concern 'education' and the challenges of teaching poetry in comprehensive schools, as a writer's life. That's a long way from Gerald Morgan's vehement editorial from 1968 demanding that Welsh poets undermine the Investiture of Prince Charles as Prince of Wales by any means possible.

To concentrate on 'political poetry' in this Introduction would be to mislead, but the grounding political impulse of *Poetry Wales* must be honoured. However, in Wales as elsewhere, political poetry declined proportionally with faith that political activism might influence events or instigate change. In the early days, poets, including the magazine's founder, Meic Stephens, contested parliamentary elections. (Mike Jenkins was still doing this as late as 1997.) But today, writers seem only too aware of what disillusionment awaits if the object of struggle is achieved: think Welsh Language Board 'official' bilingualism; the Wales Assembly Government; rule by Blairite New Labour. But if new writers look at these and deem them disappointing, perhaps they do not appreciate the struggle it took to create a devolutionary Wales.

Poetry Wales's greatest achievements are that it allows and encourages people to write. It demands that people read. Its very existence enables art to happen and debate to flourish. Can more be asked of a literary magazine?

And its greatest mistake? Looking at the evidence of 150 issues, the magazine has acted as a comfort zone for certain writers. Publishing in *Poetry Wales* is deemed enough. It is, after all, a 'national' magazine. What else is there to aspire to? *Poetry Wales* is the peak. But if a writer believes that he or she is in trouble.

Four decades after that first issue, Welsh society is almost unrecognisable. In 2005 there are far more writers than in 1965, although almost none come from where I might have expected – the English-speaking Valleys with their radical traditions and problematic present. A high proportion of the poetry I have received as the magazine editor since 1997 is written instead by those who have recently migrated to Wales. Moreover, the contemporary English language poetry scene here is diminished by the fact that many of the younger and most vigorous Welsh writers live outside the country, with little evidence that they will or can return. But this is hardly a new situation.

Also at present there is no appetite for debate about what constitutes English language culture in Wales. That question is put aside. Undoubtedly it will be readdressed. The current watchword is 'inclusivity', the mood amongst the younger writers confident, the ethos aspirational. And with the literary arts institutionalised and, yes, professionalised, by the creative writing industry, poetry with its culture of teaching and public readings is now seen as a career choice. Indeed, whether they like it or not, the phenomenon of creative writing has influenced almost all poets. In the period since *Poetry Wales – 25 Years* this has been the most profound literary development in Wales. In that time we've also seen the emergence of the bilingually productive poet (Gwyneth Lewis) – at present a singularity, but perhaps a cultural harbinger. Meanwhile, considering that *Poetry Wales* was created in 'the Valleys' largely by Valley people, the inexplicable literary inertia of those unique communities throughout much of the magazine's life must be a source of regret.

This volume takes as epigraph a poem from Kathryn Gray, a young Welsh writer not otherwise represented here. ('The Anglo-Welsh Canon' did not appear in *Poetry Wales*.) Whether "the cant of the great and good who never made us famous" is to be found in these pages, the reader will decide, but any editor will maintain that cant has its uses. But content must speak for itself. And maybe Kathryn Gray is telling us that a vigorous literature cannot be built on apology (for not being 'more Welsh'), nostalgia, or a maudlin sense of psychic 'exile' any more than it can on servility.

Inevitably, poetry comes first in this volume. But also included are examples of what I call 'the poet's essay', a 'genre' encouraged during my editorship. Thus Pascale Petit describes a childhood in mid-Wales. When political poetry was at its most vibrant here – the 1960s – Petit evokes a household where the concerns could not have been more different. And Richard Gwyn writes as a literary drifter, concerned with languages and cultures beyond his own. In their own way they contribute to a magazine which, to exist in a globalised world's lobscouse of cultures, cannot afford to cease developing. Indeed it must contain within itself that anti-Poetry Wales *Poetry Wales* as much as the *cylchgrawn cenedlaethol o farddoniaeth newydd* present since the beginning.

Robert Minhinnick May, 2005

Harri Webb

The Boomerang in the Parlour

Will Webb, a farmer's son from the cliffs of Gower,
Went as a young man to Australia, exchanging
The cramped peninsula for the outback, the frugal
Patchwork of fields for the prodigal spaces he rode
Along the rabbit-fence or under the soaring jarra.
When he came back, he brought with him a boomerang
For the front-room mantelpiece, a spearhead chipped by an
                                                    abo
From the green glass of a beer-bottle, an emu-skin rug
And the poems of Banjo Patterson. To me, his son,
He looked for the completion of a journey
Stopped at Gallipoli, that in my turn I'd see
The river of black swans. The map of Australia
Was tattooed on his right arm.
                        And so I have
Another, hypothetical, Australian self,
The might-have-been man of a clean, new, empty country
Where nearly all the songs have yet to be sung.
It is this shadow that perhaps has led me
Past islands of enchantment, capes that could have been
Called deception, disappointment and farewell,
To the strange and silent shores where now I stand:
Terra Incognita, a land whose memory
Has not begun, whose past has been forgotten
But for a clutter of legends and nightmares and lies.
This land, too, has a desert at its heart.

Tony Conran
Rhydcymerau

Near Rhydcymerau,
On the land of Esgeir-ceir and the fields of Tir-bach,
They have planted the saplings,
                              trees for the third war.
I call to mind my grandmother at Esgeir-ceir
As she sat, pleating her apron, by the fireside,
The skin yellow and dry on her face
                    like a manuscript of Peniarth,
And the Welsh on her old lips the Welsh of Pantycelyn.
A bit of the Puritan Wales she was of the last century.
Although I never saw him, my grandfather
Was a character, a brisk and jovial little creature,
Fond of his pint;
He'd just strayed in from the Eighteenth Century.
They reared nine children,
Poets, deacons, and Sunday School teachers,
And each a leader in the local community.

My Uncle Dafydd used to farm Tir-bach,
And was a country poet and a local rhymester;
His song to the little cockerel was famous in those parts:
                         "The little cock goes scratching
                              In the garden here and there."
It was to him I went for summer holidays
To watch the sheep and fashion lines of *cynghanedd*,
Englynion, and eight-line stanzas of eight-seven measure.
He also brought up eight children,
The eldest son a minister with the Calvinistic Methodists,

And he too wrote verses,
In our family we'd a real nestful of poets.

And by this time there's nothing there but trees,
With their impertinent roots sucking the old soil:
Trees where neighbourhood was,

A forest that once was farmland.
Where was verse-writing and theology
                              is the South's bastardized English.
The fox barks where once cried lambs and children,
And there in the dark midst,
Is the den of the English minotaur;
And on the trees, as if on crosses,
The bones of poets, deacons, ministers, and teachers of
                              Sunday School

Bleach in the sun,
And the rain washes them, and the winds lick them dry.

Translated from the Welsh of D. Gwenallt Jones.

Leslie Norris

Elegy for Lyn James

I saw your manager fight. He was
Useful, but his brother had the class.
In shabby halls in Wales, or in tents
On slum ground, I saw your like
Go cuffed and bleeding from a few
Crude rounds to set the mob aloud
Before the big men came, who had the class.

Even they did not all escape. Tim
Sheehan, whose young heart burst
In a dirty room above a fish shop;
Jerry O'Neill bobbing his old age
Through a confusion of scattered
Fists all down the High Street; brisk
Billy Rose, blind; all these I knew.

And Jock McAvoy, swinging his right
From a wheel-chair. Your murderers hide

Fatly behind the black lines of the
Regulations, your futile hands are closed
In a gloveless death. In rotting lanes
Behind the silent billiard halls, I hear
Your shuffling ghost, who never had the class.

Harri Webb
Epil y Filiast

Already something of a stranger now
A spry old man is walking his milgi out
Of a Sunday morning when the nineteenth century
Is in chapel and the twentieth in bed.
But his morning is centuries younger than these
As he steps it out and the lean dog lopes beside him
To fields where it will flash and pounce and double
As once in Glyn Cuch Woods.
And the old man stands in his grubby mackintosh
With a jaunty set to his shoulders,
A clean white scarf around his withered throat
And his cap on one side – ticyn slic.
His whistle carries further than the rotting pitheads,
The grass-grown tips, the flashy, flimsy estates.
He is a gambler, a drinker, a doggy-boy,
Better at drawing the dole than earning a wage.
The supermarket rises where Calfaria stood,
To him it is all one, he is older than any of it.
Mark him well, he is the last of his kind,
The last heir of Cadwaladr, Caswallon
And all our dead princes.

The Stone Face
(discovered at Deganwy, Spring 1966)

It may of course be John his father-in-law,
Their worst, our best not easily discernible
After so many buried centuries. The experts
Cannot be sure, that is why they are experts.
But this stone face under broken crown
Is not an impersonal mask of sovereignty;
This is the portrait of a living man
And when his grandson burnt Deganwy down
So that no foreign army should hold its strength
I think they buried the head of Llywelyn Fawr
As primitive magic and for reasons of state.

No fortress was ever destroyed so utterly
As was Deganwy by Llywelyn the Last,
The thoroughness of despair, foreknown defeat,
Was in the burning and breaking of its walls.
But at some door or window a hand paused,
A raised crowbar halted by the stare
Of a stone face. The Prince is summoned
And the order given: bury it in the earth,
There will be other battles, we'll be back—
Spoken in the special Welsh tone of voice
Half banter, half blind fervour, the last look
Exchanged between the hunted living eyes
And dead majesty for whom there are no problems,

The burning of Deganwy, the throne and fortress
Of Llywelyn Fawr shattered, his principality
Gone in the black smoke drifting over Menai
And his last heir forced into endless retreat.
To the banks of Irfon and the final lance-thrust.
There was no return, no reverent unearthing.

A stone face sleeps beneath the earth
With open eyes. All history is its dream.
The Great Orme shepherds the changing weather,
On Menai's shores the tides and generations
Ebb, grumble and flow; harps and hymns
Sound and fall silent; briefly the dream flares out of the eyes
Then darkness comes again.

Seven hundred and fifty years of darkness.
Now in a cold and stormy spring we stand
At the unearthing of the Sovereign head,
The human face under the chipped crown.
Belatedly, but not too late, the rendezvous is made.
The dream and the inheritors of the dream,
The founder and father, and those who must rebuild
The broken fortresses, re-establish the throne
Of eagles, here exchange the gaze of eagles
In the time of the cleansing of the eyes.

Tony Conran

Trouble at a Tavern

I came to a choice city
With my fine squire behind me.
At gay cost I ordered food
(Proud I had been from childhood)
At a worthy enough hostel—
Liberally; and wine as well.

I spied a slim fair virgin
(My sweet spirit) at that inn.
On that bright-as-dawn sweetheart
Soon I'd wholly set my heart.
A roast—not to boast!—and costly
Wine I bought for her and me.
Youth loves good cheer. I called her

(How shy she was!) to dinner,
And whispered—I dared the trick,
That's certain—two words of magic.
I made—love wasn't idle—
Tryst to come to the spry girl
As soon as all our muster
Slept; black the brows she'd on her.

When at last, wretched journey!
All did sleep, save her and me,
I to reach the lady's bed
Most skillfully attempted.
But I fell, noised it abroad,
Tumbled brutally forward.
It's easier to be clumsy,
Rising from such grief, than spry!
Nor was my leap unhurtful:
On a stupid and loud stool,
Ostler's work, to the chagrin
Of my leg, I barked my shin;
Came up, a sorry story,
And struck—may Welshmen love me!
Too great desire is evil,
Every step unlucky still!—
By blows in mad bout betrayed,
On a table-top my forehead,
Where, all the time, a pitcher
And a loud brass cauldron were.
Collapse of that stout table—
Two trestles downed—stools as well!
Cry that the cauldron uttered
Behind me, for miles was heard;
Pitcher shouted my folly,
And the dogs barked around me.

In a foul bed, at the wall,
Bothered for their packs, and fearful,
Three English lay in panic—

Hichin and Jenkin and Jack.
The young one spluttered a curse
And hissed forth to the others:

"There's a Welshman on the prowl!"
—O hot ferment of betrayal—
"He'll rob us, if we let him!
Look out you're not a victim!"

The ostler roused all the rest—
My plight was of the direst!
All round me they were angry
And searched for me all round me.
I stood, in the foul havoc
Of rage, silent in the dark;
Prayed, in no reckless fashion,
Hiding like a frightened man:
And such power has prayer for us.
Such the true grace of Jesus.
I found my own bed safe and sure
Though without sleep or treasure.
Thank the Saints, freed of distress.
I ask now God's forgiveness.

Translated from the Welsh of Dafydd ap Gwilym (fl. 1340-70)

Raymond Garlick
Capitals

Moscow,
like a Christmas-tree,
glisters on the linen snow.
Fabergé red stars filigree
the mast-high spires, glitter and flow
over the square's starched sea
below.

Madrid,
a fortress on a height,
chessboard of stone, a granite grid
lifted and spread to the lancing light
staring down from the sun's arched lid:
of Europe's cities knight
and Cid.

Dublin,
in a Yeatsian haze,
Liffey water strong as gin,
back-streets like a Chinese maze,
and Trinity, a palanquin—
the Book of Kells ablaze
within.

And Rome,
the white and marble rose
of Europe, rising from the foam
of all the fountains art unfroze
from conduits in time's catacomb:
which in their spray disclose
the dome.

Paris,
and the Seine's long psalm
holding in parenthesis
hundred-tapered Notre Dame—
pavilion of the genesis
of joy, and heaven's calm
chrysalis.

And Bonn,
empalaced on the Rhine,
where Beethoven looked out upon
symphonic counties – palatine.
Over river, bridge and swan
that fierce gaze, leonine,
once shone.

Cardiff
swirls about the numb
and calm cube of its castle cliff:
rune of departed power for some
to others towers a hieroglyph
of sovereign power to come
if if.

And last,
sun-ambered Amsterdam—
the churning hurdy-gurdy's blast
chiming with carillon and tram:
canal and concrete here contrast
their tenses, and enjamb
the past.

Europe:
young Ap Iwan's yard,
Gruffydd Robert's vision's scope,
Morgan Llwyd's hoist petard:
source to which our ballads grope—
context, compass-card
and hope.

John Idris Jones
Welsh Voices ed. Bryn Griffiths

THIS BOOK – WHICH comes with a bunch of daffodils on the dust-jacket for the traditionalists – contains a selection from the work of nineteen poets. The poets vary in age from David Jones, born in 1895, to Meic Stephens, 1938. The list of contents reveals an unexpected spread of work. Glyn Jones has only two poems, Vernon Watkins four and Raymond Garlick only two. On the other hand Sally Roberts has seven poems, John Tripp six and Dannie Abse six.

In his Introduction, the editor, Bryn Griffiths, writes that the first anthology of Anglo-Welsh poetry, *Welsh Poets,* edited by A.G. Prys-Jones, appeared in 1917; the second, *Modern Welsh Poetry*, edited by Keidrych Rhys, came in 1944, and that this present volume "is a selection of work, by living Anglo-Welsh poets, written since that time." The editor says, later: "Those poems I *have* chosen, however, seem to me representative of the best work written by Anglo-Welsh poets during the last twenty years." There is a difficulty here: what if the "best work" has been written by people who are now dead...? Even though the Introduction to this book may not be as coherent as we would like it to be, certainly the Editor's choice of material is consistent with his stated purposes (all these poets are alive). Whether these poems really are – or are representative of – the best work written in the last twenty years is a different matter. It does seem a pity that Dylan Thomas should have been omitted because of this 'still alive' rule, when people who are considerably older than he would be are included.

The editor says in the Introduction that the renaissance in Anglo-Welsh verse, which is apparently increasing in momentum, was "fostered by the foundation in 1964 of the Welsh Writers' Guild." Apart from the fact that any movement which is fostered by a guild, union or club is immediately suspect as a genuine literary phenomenon, it is common knowledge that the so-called Welsh Writers' Guild is a small group of Welshmen in London which does not seem to operate very effectively even as a cover for a social evening. Certainly, however, the advent of *Poetry Wales* has been genuinely helpful and significant, even if the work it has printed has been somewhat catholic and has not been limited so as to educe specifically Welsh or specifically new verse qualities.

The editor refers to "this new energy and vigour." It is here that this collection comes into its own. But what it shows, surely, is that this new quality which is now coming out of the most recent Anglo-Welsh verse, and which is in only some of these poems, is exciting and important because, having *less* energy and vigour, it is more in the Welsh tradition.

It is a tone-of-voice which comes out of Dylan Thomas' later poems, with their superb lyrical quality and tone of mature disillusion: it owes nothing to his earlier energetic rhetorical excesses. What seems to me to be in the poetry of John Tripp, Sally Roberts and Herbert Williams especially, as represented here, is a Voice which is reminiscent of Hedd Wyn and Ceiriog. It is a combination of aesthetic form, of clarity and maturity, of a determination to tell the truth, of concern with subjects which are actual and real, and of intelligence.

This is the new note which one can only regret that this collection did not reveal more adequately: but it is a very recent development. For those who have been reading *The Anglo-Welsh Review*, this Voice has been there for a number of years in the work of Raymond Garlick, Roland Mathias, Valerie Minogue, John Stuart Williams and Peter Preece. It has however been overly 'aesthetic,' which is perhaps to a degree due to the work of Vernon Watkins, who has been occupying a rather brittle aesthetic limb for a long time; at least to the Yeatsian Watkins and not, unfortunately, to that strain in his work responsible for the fine poem *The Collier*. Certainly this new note owes much to R. S. Thomas, whose deeply serious, astringent poems of massive integrity have stood out of the general ruck of Anglo-Welsh writing during the last ten years rather like a lighthouse which points the way ahead because it itself is founded on solid ground. The new Voice which we hear in many of the poems in this anthology is a testimony to the struggles of many writers who are attempting to find a middle way between the highly individual rhetoric of Dylan Thomas and the ordered and rather predictable cadences of R.S. Thomas. This way is undoubtedly being laid down now, but it does need a greater variety in subject and technique, a greater sophistication of method, and more wit and humour before it can reach a satisfying literary maturity.

If one were to trace the degree of artistic pleasure which reading this collection gives, it would start at a high point with the work of Dannie Abse and proceed generally downwards, with the occasional upsurge: but this is largely to say that one's disappointment increases as one reads on and the comparative similarity of the subjects and methods employed in this verse tells on one's critical judgement. If only there was a funny poem... a very short, precise poem... poems which showed a real awareness of new tendencies in American verse. One would like more of the sort of thing William Carlos Williams at his best does so well: it may merely be a matter of painting a little picture in words, but to do that well is difficult; this American sense of the immediate, of the sensory present, would be an antidote to our Welsh tendency to be 'heavy,' explicit and didactic. When we turn away from music, which is the Welshness in us, we tend to fall too easily into the prosaic. I see the selections from David Jones' poetry in this way because their effect relies on intellectual meaning rather than upon sound and rhythm. And the following, for instance, is really prose put into lines:

Will Webb, a farmer's son from the cliffs of Gower,
Went as a young man to Australia, exchanging
The cramped peninsula for the outback, the frugal
Patchwork of fields for the prodigal spaces he rode
Along the rabbit-fence or under the soaring jarrah.

This tendency descends into doggerel in the poem *The Wife of Carcassone:*

...so she grew thinner.
As thin, in fact, as any lath.
And one sad evening, in her bath
She slipped and slithered down the vent
Calling her husband as she went.
But he, alas, not understanding,
Stood wavering upon the landing.

There are no good poets, only good poems. Let's look at some of the poems, in the order in which they are printed.

Dannie Abse's *Epithalamion* is remarkable for its controlled richness and for the successful slight alterations in each stanza's last lines; but despite its undeniable beauty its subject is difficult to follow, containing many lines where the imagery and meaning is very compressed. When the meaning is not so clotted, as at the end of 'Return to Cardiff', the effect is very impressive:

> No sooner than I'd arrived the other Cardiff had gone,
> smoke in the memory, these but tinned resemblances,
> where the boy I was not and the man I am not
> met, hesitated, left double footsteps, then walked on.

Raymond Garlick's 'Still Life' is a successful attempt to 'paint a picture in words': its skilful use of verbs and separation of detail amount almost to a re-enactment of the action of the painter.

The editor, Bryn Griffiths, has, I think, represented himself poorly with his two poems 'The Shadow Beasts' and 'The Dead March'. The former is formless, repetitious and overly personal, whilst the latter seems to strike a false attitude. There are better poems than these in the author's first collection *The Mask of Pity*, and one also thinks of 'Singleton Pool' published recently in *Country Quest*.

In 'Old Nosey', which comes after the attitudinising of 'Eisteddfod', Peter Gruffydd shows that when he concentrates on detail rather than ideas he writes with precision and power:

> Like a squirrel but not so efficient,
> Piling speculation, working, glancing,
> Noting, quick as a bird to a crumb,
> Grab – gone in a dart, stored, noted,
> But who watches her – no one.
> No one watches: her whole boned life
> In this one street and its carnival
> Of drip-dry sins...

I am sorry to say that I have little sympathy with David Jones' work, as represented here: for me, this particular emperor has no clothes. I find it difficult to sympathise with such arcane mediaevalising when all around us there are so many serious subjects to write about. He resembles Ezra Pound and T.S. Eliot, but I can find in his work only little of the music of the former and none of the social insight of the latter.

The selections from Roland Mathias' work show a rather timid flatness, except for 'Departure in Middle Age', which is direct and very moving:

> They are all dead, all,
> Or scattered, father, mother, my pinafore friends,
> And the playground's echoes have not waited for my return.
> Exile is the parcel I carry , and you know this,
> Clouds, when you drop your pretences and the hills clear.

Robert Morgan's poems '4C Boy' and 'Maladjusted Boys' are both successful because they stay very close to the subject, but when he writes about miners the depiction is vicarious and smacks of a clouding retrospection. The repetitiveness of his collier themes is mixed with some rather tired figurative language:

> So if our tongues are blunt and our hands
> Screwed by the vice of crude work,
> Then remember, these are only grains
> Hiding the encounter with the soul's landscape.

Leslie Norris is, surely, badly represented. It is difficult to see how the same author could write lines such as, "hearing the nightingale / Hammer my plaintive rest with remorseless melody. / Full of resented ecstasy, I groaned nightlong in my bed," and also some of the poems in his recent Triskel Press collection.

Sally Roberts' work reveals a truly individual voice which speaks honestly and clearly out of deeply felt experience. 'A Small Tragedy' is an outstanding poem: through its sparse structure and carefully-chosen details it reveals the horror of a dehumanised life:

> In the end, of course,
> He was hanged,
> Very neatly,
> Though pleading insanity.
> A quiet little man,
> Who knew what to do with files and paper-clips,
> But had no ideas about people
> Except to destroy them.

Also 'Daws Hill' and 'Earthquake' are fine poems with very powerful endings. One feels in each of these poems by Sally Roberts that here is a finely-tuned artistic intelligence which is shaping its material with increasing assurance.

Meic Stephens' 'Old Timers' is less successful than his 'Ponies, Twynyrodyn' because the subject is presented rather than described: the latter poem is a good one, containing sensory details which carry the symbolism with deftness. 'Old Timers' is heavy with Welshness.

Of R.S. Thomas' new poems, 'Llanrhaeadr-Ym-Mochnant' and 'Where to Go' stand out. About Bishop Morgan's great work in translating the Bible into Welsh in this "village in North Wales," as the editor rather off-handedly puts it, the Rev. Thomas writes:

> The smooth words
> Over which his mind flowed
> Have become an heirloom. Beauty
> Is how you say it, and the truth,
> Like this mountain-born torrent,
> Is content to hurry
> Not too furiously by.

The end of the latter poem is equally impressive in its intellectual penetration and power of simple statement:

> Where can I go, then, from the smell
> Of decay, from the putrefying of a dead
> Nation? I have walked the shore
> For an hour, and seen the English
> Scavenging among the remains
> Of our culture, covering the sand
> Like the tide, and with the roughness
> Of the tide elbowing our language
> Into the grave that we have dug for it.

Something has happened to John Tripp's work. Suddenly he is writing in a new and effective way. 'Separation' is a very moving poem, full of urgent honesty; it works so well partly because the author has not focussed too sharply on his subject. By pulling away from the separation – "I will watch another sunset... another dawn..." – he manages to communicate a sense of mature perspective which gives the poem real stature. There is a strong sense of the reality of every-day living in this poem which one wishes was more of in the rest of this book. This is certainly one of the best poems here.

Herbert Williams is also writing with a new power, with a new compelling quietness. 'The Inheritor' communicates helplessness and courage equally; it is a moving poem on a subject which must have been both emotionally and artistically difficult to handle. Both 'The Castle Choir' and 'The Old Tongue' communicate valid aspects of our Welsh predicament. The end of the latter has that new note I have referred to:

> Oh yes, there have been gains.
> I merely state
> That the language, for us,
> Is part of the old, abandoned ways.
> And when I hear it, regret
> Disturbs me like a requiem.

Finally, the selection from John Stuart Williams' work is hardly adequate. 'Maud Gonne' is a good poem, neatly turned and precise: 'Skokholm' shows the author's ability to communicate the Mediterranean type of landscape and sense of space, and 'Exile' shows an intellectual awareness:

> Now, pedantic and precise
> In a foreign tongue, you tap your nervous
> Cigarette, tilt your head
> Like one who knows his role – a poet
> In a strange, prosaic land –
> And talk of the country left behind;
> Still in love with dreams you do
> Not now believe, lost in the sharp
> Entanglements of time and place.

Many of the poets in this book are articulating the tragedy of Wales, following R.S. Thomas. But as well as "worrying the carcase of an old song" they are building a new song upon the foundations of the old. We must be grateful to Mr Bryn Griffiths for engineering the publication of this book, which shows the direction in which the really new verse is going. If

Anglo-Welsh poets continue to write as well, with as much artistry, honesty and reality, as some of the poets in this book, then we can expect that they will make a significant contribution to the sum of British poetry written in the late 60's and the 70's.

Gerald Morgan

The Penguin Book of Welsh Verse ed. Anthony Conran

THE UNATTACHED READER of this anthology may well be envied – he will only be concerned to gain some idea of the range and quality of Welsh poetry. For the Welsh reader, and especially the Welsh-reading reader, it is a far more complicated matter. We know we haven't yet got much in the way of art and sculpture, or even music, but *myn diawl* we've got our poetry, the peak of our achievement, and everybody's missing a lot through not being able to read it.

It becomes a matter of status, a proof of our nationality and of our language's worth, a matter of urgency. Consequently there was rejoicing when Principal Thomas Parry produced his *Oxford Book of Welsh Verse*, not because it was the first comprehensive anthology of Welsh poetry (to the shame of his predecessors) and a monumental piece of work, but because it was an "Oxford book," meaning that Welsh was recognised along with English, German, French, etc. However, since only Welsh-readers could tackle it, our claims were not wholly satisfied. *The Penguin Book of Welsh Verse* will be received as another brick laid in the cause of Welsh status; the next brick must be a Nobel Prize.

Actually, extraordinary as it may seem, Mr Conran has had more help from his predecessors than had Principal Parry. Few and hopelessly incomplete were the anthologies of Welsh poetry, whereas Mr Conran's predecessors have made respectable efforts to smooth his path. Published translation from Welsh poetry to English began in the eighteenth century with the work of Thomas Gray and Evan Evans on the early poetry, and has continued sporadically ever since. Usually goodwill has been more evident than ability, and too often the taut music of Welsh became an English jingle, notorious proof of Robert Frost's dictum – "Poetry is what is lost in translation."

However, in recent years quality too has improved, notably in the work of Professors Gwyn Jones and T.J. Morgan (on the Llywarch Hen poems), Professor Joseph Clancy (on the *cywyddau*) and Professor Gwyn Williams, whose four volumes, *The Rent That's Due to Love, The Burning Tree, An Introduction to Welsh Poetry* and *Presenting Welsh Poetry* have done so much to give an idea of the range and scope of Welsh poetry.

The job facing Mr Conran was a grim one. First, he had to choose his poems, a task in which it is quite impossible to satisfy anybody. Mr Conran's desire to choose the "best" poems was inevitably qualified not only by the usual problem of breadth of representation, but by whether he could trans-late them to his own satisfaction. His task was lightened by the appearance of the *Oxford Book*, on which he obviously depended for support in some difficult periods.

Although the Penguin book had to be much shorter than the Oxford, I find that sometimes Mr Conran was able to improve on the latter's choice. I prefer the Penguin choice of Williams Parry and Gwenallt, and I think it gives a better account of Gwalchmai as a poet – in fact, the choice from the Court Poets generally is an improvement. In the choice of Guto'r Glyn, Parry Williams and Saunders Lewis, I prefer Oxford, and I note Penguin's omission of Tudur Aled, Sion Phylip, Anne Griffiths and Bobi Jones with surprise.

Penguin is thin in the late eighteenth century, too, and it is interesting to weigh the two sets of modern poems – Oxford over-generous in its choice of names, Penguin rather miserly. Obviously, however, Penguin is in Oxford's debt not merely for guidance in choice of authors and poems, but for the determination by that choice of the nature of the anthology. The Oxford Book emphasises the continuity and historical tradition, the sense of form in Welsh poetry, qualities which obviously appeal strongly to Mr Conran.

Given his choice, Mr Conran's work had hardly begun. The danger facing a single translator covering a wide period is that poets from widely different periods will be represented in the same style; I feel this to be a weakness in *The Burning Tree*, for example. Yet we can't translate Taliesin into Anglo-Saxon and Gwenallt into Swansea Valley English; every poet must be given a twentieth century dress, and yet retain his individuality.

Almost all the time Mr Conran succeeds in this difficult job; the terseness of the ancients:

> Cold bed of fish in the gloom of ice;
> Stag lean, bearded reeds;
> Evening brief, slant of bent wood.

and the deliberate slackness of Gwenallt:

> Near Rhydycymerau
> On the land of Esgeir-ceir and the fields of Tir-bach,
> They have planted the saplings
> to be trees of the third war.

are both achieved (though I think "the wood" might be better than "trees").

These problems are those of any translator of poetry, but in the case of Welsh, we have the problem of form. Classical Welsh poetry is aural poetry; allliteration, internal rhyme, accent, rhyme, repetition and syllable-count are essential to it, whether in the lengthy *cywydd* or the brief *englyn*. Mr Conran has decided to keep the shape of his originals as far as possible; usually syllable for syllable exactly, rhyme as far as possible, and a trace of alliteration when achievable.

In the *cywydd* I feel he has achieved marvels. Often indeed a fine couplet may be weakened in translation, but the over-all effect is musical, vivid and accurate. He sometimes exploits the Welsh-rhyme of the *cywydd* excellently, e.g.

> The good crops of the white flesh
> In the earth blacken and perish

where the falling rhyme musically creates the sense of the couplet despite the loss of *cynghanedd*. The loss of the richness of texture in the *cywyddau* is compensated for by the new sense gained of the shape of the poems as wholes.

The *englynion*, however, are another matter. When they are in chains, the accumulative effect works well enough, but those splendid individual stanzas with their incredible complexity and terseness are ruined in translation.

It's pleasant to look homeward

is an accurate translation of the sense of

Teg edrych tuag adref

but everything else is lost, and there is no compensation.

Perhaps the finest feat of this volume is the collection of poems by the *Gogynfeirdd*, the poets of the Princes of independent Wales. This is I feel because of the special gift which Mr Conran brings to his work. He is himself a poet, with a prodigious English vocabulary, to whom English words are gems, to be cut by their context to their finest shape and brilliance. In his own original work, however, this gift seemed to lack definition – there were gems, but no crown. Definition has come with the imposition of the translator's work, just as an actor is most himself when recreating the character of another.

The *Gogynfeirdd* were such poets, assemblers of phrases which strike sparks from each other:

I call down God's protection – sure your gifts
  And I your gifted one –
  On your warriors, war-eagle.
  On your land, lord of the South.

Of all Welsh poets they are the most "other" to us; knotty, arrogant, bellicose, far more remote and difficult to tackle than the more ancient work of Aneirin and the saga poems, yet obviously with a special appeal to the translator.

Mr Conran's long introduction is also a considerable achievement; I find it provocative, civilised and almost entirely brilliant and convincing, especially on the *cywydd* tradition.

I hope that *Poetry Wales* will follow this review with the

reaction of someone knowing no Welsh. I can't help reading many of these translations with the music of the original in my mind, and the organ music of the original tends to sound like a piano in translation, skilfully though it is played. Indeed, I am afraid the skill may deceive readers into feeling that there is nothing to be gained by making the effort to understand the originals, whereas Mr Conran himself must hope that his work will challenge people to wrestle with the original. His splendid achievement is a passport to a poetic tradition unique in Europe, justified not only by its antiquity and its "otherness," but simply by its quality. Not only does this volume represent a body of fine poetry, but there is plenty more where it came from, and to the shame of the Welsh, there is still some in manuscript, unpublished. To Mr Conran and his Bangor helpers, and to the pyramid of pioneers and contemporaries on whose shoulders he stands (especially those Welsh scholars who made accurate translations of the ancient poetry possible), our thanks. I do not believe the job will be better done in our time.

John Tripp
The Province of Belief

Why it should be given
to this small land, this narrow sleeve like Israel,
to bury a secret,
    I do not know.
Yet it is there. As if somewhere
rooted out of two thousand years
the truth hides in the cracks
of chapels, in the tilted graves
stark on the evening skyline
above the decimated villages.
    (You would say
this place deserved better
if you knew of its disfiguring past.)

Here the kinder side of history
turned away, leaving these people
stranded on a tide of silver,
trudging to their bony faith,
keeping union with God's promise
of Caersalem beyond this dirt.
Here our hot little plans and appetites
buckle under the ruins of prayer,
far from the clanging townships
and the drag of the conveyor belts.
  Always through the clocking seasons
in Wales I clearly see
the botch of our desires,
the scrabbling rush to havoc
and the scratched yields of our lives
as the last sad threads of faith's remnant
unravel a glimpse of eternity.

Gerald Morgan & Gwilym Rees Hughes
Editorial *Gwrth-Groeso '69*

SO WELSH MUSICIANS have been castrated. With one blast every well-known Welsh composer and singer has lined up to perform at Caernarfon. How ominous then is the silence where Welsh writers are concerned. Not a word of a commission so far – though of course I may be found wrong before we come from the press. Has someone ratted? Who has told the Duke of Norfolk that almost every Welsh-language writer of note is a member of Plaid Cymru? Is Cynan polishing his last Awdl? Will John Eilian versify his pukeful editorials in *Yr Herald Cymraeg*?

Since Plaid Cymru has shown itself in such a lily-livered light and even *Cymdeithas yr Iaith Gymraeg* is leaving its protest until next March 1st. I suggest that the Welsh Academy should announce a Gwrth-Groeso (Anti-Welcome) in time for writers' competitions and commissions to be organised. Dafydd Iwan's "Carlo" song should be printed in broadsheet form and sold for a penny a time. Satirical odes should be commissioned from Harri Webb (in English) and Gwenallt (in Welsh). There should be a pop-song competition, with recording guaranteed. More seriously, a historian could be commissioned to produce a booklet, *The Princes of Wales*. Each left-hand page would carry a biographical sketch of one of the historical kings and princes of Wales before 1282 (plus Glyndwr). The right-hand page would carry a similar sketch of one of the English (or Scottish or French or German) Princes of Wales. There would be no bias in the writing. Only the whole nature of the exercise would show its purpose, especially if Llywelyn Fawr were placed opposite the Prince Regent, and Llywelyn ein Llyw Olaf opposite Edward VII, with Glyndwr facing the Duke of Windsor.

Anyway, *Poetry Wales* promises that any bardic effusions on the Investiture will be given due and (despite the above) impartial consideration, the final arbiter being literary quality alone. But I think I can guess on which side the quantity, at any rate, will fall.

Leslie Norris

Ransoms

for Edward Thomas

What the white ransoms did was to wipe away
The dry irritation of a journey half across
England. In the warm tiredness of dusk they lay
Like moonlight fallen clean onto the grass,

And I could not pass them. I wound
Down the window for them and for the still
Falling dark to come in as they would,
And then remembered that this was your hill,

Your precipitous beeches, your wild garlic.
I thought of you walking up from your house
And your heartbreaking garden, melancholy
Anger sending you into this kinder darkness,

And the shining ransoms bathing the path
With pure moonlight. I have my small despair
And would not want your sadness; your truth,
Your tragic honesty, are what I know you for.

I think of a low house upon a hill,
Its door closed now even to the hushing wind
The tall grass bends to, and all the while
The far-off salmon river without sound

Runs on below; but if this vision should
Be yours or mine I do not know. Pungent
And clean the smell of ransoms from the wood,
And I am refreshed. It was not my intent

To stop on a solitary road, the night colder,
Talking to a dead man, fifty years dead,
But as I flick the key, hear the engine purr,
Drive slowly down the hill, I'm comforted.

Harri Webb
Ode to the Severn Bridge

Two lands at last connected
Across the waters wide
And all the tolls collected
On the English side.

Raymond Garlick
Map Reading

Look north if you like:
Eryri, water, Kirkudbright,
the fingers of the Arctic sun
feeling out gold on the white
plains of the pole's Klondyke.

Look south even more:
Cardiff, the Bridge, and beyond
the Summer Country, Europe
shimmering up from the pond
of the Manche like a solar shore.

The west is all right:
the sea, the Republic, the crash
and spin of the ocean, furlongs
of light; only then bulks the brash
American shore, and the night.

Best avoid the east:
below the Dyke it's getting dark
in the tangled, litter-blown
Greater London park
of Britain, deceased.

Glyn Jones
Bindweed

Suddenly the scent of bindweed in the warm lane
And the smoking sea of remembering him bursts open
Upon its rocks, its snow-dust wets the sun.

The heavy scent of bindweed brings only sorrow.
Grey gull-flocks puffed over waves disintegrate like gunsmoke.
Storm-sodden crags are not colder than my heart.

Bindweed is the scent of heavy remembering.
Beyond the window – the great ocean in its bed.
I am alone. In the past Gwyn was with me.

The scent of bindweed drifts like childhood remembered.
Meshed white on green is the great wave's polished incurve.
Bullets that took Gwyn were already in flight.

Cruel the sweet scent of innocent bindweed.
Winds tear off the tide's skin in one brandished fleece.
Gwyn died. Happiness is irrational.

Bindweed now in this lane, then in that sea-garden.
Waves everywhere throw anguished arms around rocks.
The comforter in his comforting is not comforted.

Sweet bindweed was heavy in that August garden.
The grey sea stiffens and sinks to a slab of iron.
How is it the heart dead at its quick can suffer?

R.S. Thomas
Shame

This is the botched land,
The land of a few
Rifles and home-made bombs.
The men drill in the back-yard
Of the heart, march to a dead
Music. But the police come.
The one-eyed marksman, the
Commandant blowing
His toy bugle – the world
Laughs at them. But the law
Puts laughter away. Leviathan's
Hide twitches. It tells its hurt
To the court. The jury
Is outraged. Three more men
Will suffer an iron

Clemency. In the striped flag
On the tower there is the insolence
Of a poster advertising
A nation for sale.

Harri Webb

A Crown for Branwen

I pluck now an image out of a far
Past and a far place, counties away
On the wrong side of Severn, acres
Of alien flint and chalk, the smooth hills
Subtly, unmistakeably English, different.
I remember, as if they were China, Sinodun,
Heaven's Gate and Angel Down, the White Horse
Hidden from the eye of war, Alfred at Wantage,
His bodyguard of four Victorian lamp-posts
And his country waiting for another enemy
Who did not come that summer. Everything
Shone in the sun, the burnished mail of wheat
And hot white rock, but mostly I recall
The long trench.
                     A thousand years from now
They'll find the line of it, they'll tentatively
Make scholarly conjectures relating it
To Wansdyke, the Icknield Way, Silbury.
They'll never have known a summer
Of tense expectancy that drove
A desperate gash across England
To stop the tanks.
                     Most clearly I see
The tumbled ramparts of frantic earth
Hastily thrown up, left to the drifting
Seeds of the waste, and the poppies,
Those poppies, that long slash of red
Across the shining corn, a wound, a wonder.

Lady, your land's invaded, we have thrown
Hurried defences up, our soil is raw,
New, shallow, the old crops do not grow
Here where we man the trench. I bring
No golden-armoured wheat, the delicate dance
Of oats to the harvest is not for me nor
The magic spears of barley, on this rough stretch
Only the poppies thrive. I wreathe for you
A crown of wasteland flowers, let them blaze
A moment in the midnight of your hair
And be forgotten when the coulter drives
A fertile furrow over our old wars
For the strong corn, our children's bread.
Only, princess, I ask that when you bring
Those bright sheaves to the altar, and you see
Some random poppies tangled there, you'll smile,
As women do, remembering dead love.

John Ormond

Salmon

The river sucks them home.
The lost past claims them.
    Beyond the headland
It gropes into the channel
Of the nameless sea.
    Offshore they submit
To the cast, to the taste of it.
It releases them from salt,
Their thousand miles in odyssey
For spawning. It rehearsed their return
    From the beginning; now
    It clenches them like a fist.

43

The echo of once being here
Possesses and inclines them.
    Caught in the embrace
Of nothing that is not now,
Riding in with the tide-race,
    Not by their will,
Not by any will they know,
They turn fast to the caress
Of their only course. Sea-hazards done,
They ache towards the one world
    From which their secret
    Sprang, perpetuate

More than themselves, the ritual
Claim of the river, pointed
    Towards rut, casting
Their passion out. Weeping philosopher,
They re-affirm the world,
    The stars by which they ran,
Now this precise place holds them
Again. They reach the churning wall
Of the brute waterfall that shed
Them young from its cauldron pool.
    A hundred times
    They lunge and strike

Against the hurdles of the rock;
Though hammering water
    Beats them back
Still their desire will not break.
They coil and whip and kick,
    Tensile for their truth's
Sake; give to the miracle
Of their treadmill leaping
The illusion of the natural.
The present in torrential flow
    Nurtures its own
    Long undertow:

They work it, strike and streak again,
Filaments in suspense.
     The lost past shoots them
Into flight out of their element,
In bright transilient sickle-blades
     Of light; until upon
The instant's height of their inheritance
They chance in descant over the loud
Diapasons of flood, jack out of reach
And snatch of clawing water,
     Stretch and soar
     Into easy rapids

Beyond, into half-haven, jounce over
Shelves upstream; and know no question
     But, pressed by their cold blood,
Glance through the known maze.
They unravel the thread to source
     To die at their ancestry's
Last knot, knowing no question.
They meet under hazel trees
Are chosen and so mate. In shallows as
The stream slides clear, yet shirred
     With broken surface where
     Stones trap the creamy stars

Of air, she scoops at gravel with fine
Thrust of her exact, blind tail;
     At last her lust
Gapes in a gush on her stone nest
And his great squanderous peak
     Shudders his final hunger
On her milk; seed laid on seed
In spunk of liquid silk.
So in exhausted saraband their slack
Convulsions wind and wend galactic
     Seed in seed, a found
     World without end.

The circle's set, proportion
Stands complete, and
    Ready for death
Haggard they hang in aftermath
Abundance, ripe for the world's
    Rich night, the spear.
Why does this fasting fish
So haunt me? Gautama, was it this
You saw from river-bank
At Uruvela? Was this
    Your glimpse
    Of holy law?

Raymond Garlick
England Needs You

Seven of the Welsh archers
whose arrows eclipsed the sun
in icy susurrations
when Agincourt was done
had gone there from Llansteffan.
When that day's death was won

if any of them lived
I wonder what they thought.
I live in Llansteffan
and I know Agincourt –
the bone-meal verdant meadows
over which they fought:

green places, both of them now,
but then, in 1415,
at Agincourt the blood
clotted the buttercups' sheen
and the earth was disembowelled
where stakes and hooves had been.

And far off, in Llansteffan,
castle, village and shore
flowered in the marigold sun.
Did those seven men explore
the contrast of this peace
with another English war?

Footnote

To be frank, England
is a country that I just don't know.
I was born there, of course,
in London, some forty years ago;
grew up, was schooled there,
in my fifteenth year was forced to go

to a factory there
to earn my bread. And then at eighteen
I was born again
in the granite and ultramarine
of Bangor, made free
at last of suburbia's pink patine.

That's England for me –
soliptical London, a stain
on the mind's old map;
and today, what must be crossed to gain
Dover, Southampton,
and through them Belgium, Italy, Spain

and the world one knows,
familiar contexts of French and Dutch.
England is the lost
constriction of childhood, beyond touch
and relevance now.
One can't believe one has missed much.

Glyn Jones

Where All were Good to Me, God Knows

Seeing the block of flats, I remember
The meadows under them, where Jones the Stoning's
Skewbald cart-horse would walk in sunshine among
Fluid swallows, camouflaged conspicuous
As a tank, and the Jones's white-washed house,
And their long garden with the door in the wall,
In at which squat Russ and I floated and, through
Subaqueous gloom of their glass trees, out
On to their sunlit lawn, vast and glowing.

"Welcome, come in, my boy," said Mr Jones
– A shy man, he was never in the handshake
First to remit the pressure – adding
"zzz," when he saw there were two of us.
God bless much overfed, norfolk-suited,
Green-stockinged, yellow-booted Mr Jones
– Destined for his nest, must be, I thought, that fluff
Moustache – his high collar, his high colour
Glassy, tight over his shining head
The polished membrane of his tarry hair.

And his crippled Philip also, rowdiest
Hunchback goalie in the game – I remember
His brown hair-helmet (in sunlight the red
Gravy of sea-iron), the sad faces inked
On his finger-nails, his nutmeg freckling,
The feel of crutch-pads warm from his armpits.

Bare-footed we played cards and ate apples,
While sweating Mr Jones, dumb talker,
Witty listener, sat watching us before
His red bed of flat sun-gulper tulips,
And the sun-soaked wall where deep udders
Of shadow hung down darkening the stonework –
Beaming, his fat hand nursing his fat fist.

A raft of starlings exploded off the grass,
A full thrush hopped heavily with long
Kangaroo hops down the lawn, and slowly
Mrs. Jones followed long-frocked from the dazzling
                                                        house.
God bless his beautiful Mrs. Jones also,
Her drake-head-green gown, her broad-brimmed hat,
                                                her cool
Face gold, radiant in lawn-reflected amber,
Her smile a mirror in which I smiled to see
Myself always clever, beautiful and good,
And before which bare-footed Russ blushed
Into his shirt, and aitches were the aitches
Soon, of a boy who never sounded aitches.

        Mr Jones's face turned sharp out the shadow
Towards her, smiling, and some long curved
Nostril hair suddenly lit up red, glowed hot
In sunlight like a burning filament –

        All are dead, Jones the Stoning, Mrs. Jones,
Philip, Russ, the charm, the tenderness, the glow.
Evening drops a vast sun into sunset
Where it smoulders swollen, boiling behind
The flats – once the great cart-horses pounded on
Pavings of those nightfall-slated meadows,
Where grey Danter, too, the Jones's pig-headed
Pony stood asleep beneath the burnt-out tree.
God bless beautiful flats also, I suppose.
Lights go on in windows. People live in them
And great stars flash among vanished branches
And night-owls call from elms no longer there.

Jeremy Hooker
Elegy for the Labouring Poor

1 *The picturesque*

> "There will soon be an end to the picturesque in the Kingdom." (John Constable, after the destruction, by fire, of Purns Mill.)

I

The picturesque is always with us.
Paint stiffens but the river swims forward;
Clouds move on and a mill becomes ash,
But the human features stay variable
And the pliant earth defies stasis.
And it is there, in that movement,
As another sky forms and a new generation
Measures the wood or levels the corn,
That the imagination commits itself
To an act that is elegy and salutation:
For what is welcomed – this continuity,
Is also change displacing the self that welcomes.
The carpenter alone commands a permanent living,
Elm perpetual usage. Nothing lasts
But the mortal nature of all that's unique.

II

Near Bishopstone the family tended sheep
And ploughed the flint. There I glimpsed
A tractor fuming chalkdust
And found the fields worked profitably
But empty, smooth and pallid.
I came to the village under the downs
Whose graveyard held few stones –
The rest had ended in town cemeteries
Or been put to sea. Not one
Pushed a pen or was pushed by one.

Why grub in the past
For that life whose work seems fickle as ash?

Not to savour lachrymae rerum, nor toll
The general dirge that the globe goes round,
As the elegist wags a grave skull
Sonorous as a belfry: plough fossil,
Fossil pylon...
But to resurrect from the used land
The life that gave life; to utter it
As it cannot be known in the canvas
Where river and cloud stand fast,
Or in chronicles of the cold law;
As it can only be guessed by the self
Acknowledging change; as it can never be known.

2 *Forefather*

He moves like timber on a swell,
In mud gaiters and clay-coloured cord,
Bent to it, sculpting a furrow.
Mould's his name: James Mould
With shoots in Hants and Wiltshire.
His blunt boot-prints, fugitive
As the cloud at his rear,
Are unseen by the camera which exhumes
Celtic patterns from suave downland.
But the tread's purposeful.

His prayer's a bold harvest;
That the seed will stand up golden,
As an army, as mansions in Portland oolite,
As three loaves weekly
God's ear is readier than Parliament's
Since He'll ferret in barn, byre and hen house,
Tithe-hungry.
                    So he trudges,
Chained by daylight
To the round of a stiff field,
Deaf as yet to saucy agitation.
For living it is not, but a long starving.

3 *"Gold Fever", 1830*

After nightfall in harvest weather,
Over the lowland clay
Where the axe has opened hearts of oak,
A faint wind moves in the rigging of leaves.
On the quayside at Poole
Limestone waits shipment, and Portland
With its moon-grey scars butts into the sea.
Bored by the company of sheep
White horses gallop on the ridge of chalk,
But the Cerne giant, erect through an aeon,
Dreams of slackening into repose.
– Green man, fathering riches,
Delicate in the turn of a leafy wrist
Or puckish among moon-drunk sheaves,
Subject to none but the turning year,
Now fires in the labourer's veins,
Kindling the brand – and flexes strongly,
In the fist that will quench it,
Musket and shot and the outraged warrant
Of a mastering brain...

No man's lonelier than James Mould
As he wakes with stubble-scored legs
In a rat's refuge of wattle and daub.
At first the mist hangs clammy flags
But vanishes as the sun hardens
White-hot on flint, deadening the hedgerows.
Hunger isolates: however neighboured
In a common circumstance,
The body slogs alone, by rote,
And the jailed brain dulls
Fixed on the single motion – the arcing scythe
Deliberate as the sun at its habitual act.
Thus he swings through the day, a young man
Hard and spare as the grain
Now whispering in heaps,

Bent with his shoulder to the field,
Keeping it moving, glad of the work,
At a Klondyke near Bishopstone.

4 *Captain Swing fires the workhouse*

Rag bedding indelibly staled,
Lousy straw crusted with piss –
Tinder for the pyre.

Lit, the flames flick cleanly.
Like a candle in a turnip skull
The house makes a face in the dark.
The grass slithers with rats.
Then the windows stare out,
Splintering, and the fire explodes.
To a shepherd out on the downs
It's a cauldron fed by the oak,
As it ruins suddenly, lustily,
And the walls wither and the roof falls,
Pounding down timber and stone.
Like a yule log
It flickers on the watchful old.

Where's Swing?
The sergeant barks at his redcoats.
The magistrate chokes on latinate prose.

No one knows
Not even a score of labourers
Cat-footing it through the underwood;
Among them, James Mould,
Daredevil as a boy again,
Pleased with himself and scared.

5 *The voyage out, 1831*

Bladder-wrack swaying in supple knots
Muddies the sunned quayside water.
Each for itself and each self

Viciously alike, the black-headed gulls
Snatch at refuse, and their raw cries
Spread in circles, smacking the hulk,
Thinning out where the estuary opens
And the sea absorbs their voice.
But James Mould seeing the ocean
Sees only flint acres
Fought inch by inch, chalkdust rising,
And hears only his ghostly kin
Telling their names in the stunned brain.

When Portland pitches astern
And the last gull's torn shoreward,
Memory stays. The hulk bores on,
Shuddering, and the massive slabs break,
The clean fathomless wells slide open.
But the waves have faces
And the unbroken space narrows
To an inland patch of fields,
The chalk ridge, the sheep-walk scabius.

For this is purgation: to scour men
By divorcing them from all they know.
But the things they love go with them,
Untouchable, at times ferociously clear.
And what's left pleads after them,
And sours. Places are empty
That nothing but bitterness can fill.
The labourer voyages. The land uses
New methods, new men. But he takes with him
A life belonging to those acres
And leaves as a portion, the emptiness.
Under the downs, in countless sites
Gutted by the exile of their people,
Others will meet this isolation.
They will inherit the emptiness.

Tony Conran
Fern Frond
for John Wain

Why don't I send you
A fern really old –
Osmunda, with its massive
Stump-like bole?

Marattia or *Anigiopteris–*
Squat little trees
That through the millennia
Inched down by degrees –

Dowagers of the rain forests
Left to their plight
In the hundred yard high
Struggle for light –

Or *Lygodium,* the last
Climbing fern –
Queens that hark back to a realm
Of no return?

No, the Ghost Dance is over.
Redskin encampment
Knows no more dreams. Paleface
Magic's too rampant.

Not even suicide, not even
A fight to the death.
Only the necessity
Not to waste breath.

Only the immutable gene
Sullen beyond fear,
Only the getting drunk
On white man's beer.

No, John, this is a frond
Quite other than those
That were ousted by a flower
From Eden groves.

Evolved, sophisticated,
Able to hold
Its own where it chooses to be,
Withstanding the cold

Of our British winters
Like any birch or oak.
Red leaf burns on the hill.
Red dreams turn to smoke.

This fern has no royal blood –
Or if it has,
Only as much as is green
In a blade of grass.

Long after the Battle of the Trees
Was lost, and flowers
And fruits began to flaunt
Imperial powers,

Creating for their use
Insect, beast and bird,
Learning the way of quick returns –
Decay and rebirth:

Long after that, in an Atlantis
Buried under the snows –
A lost Antarctic world –
Before the ice floes

Clanged to about it, and all
That was left
Of the whole teeming continent
Was blizzard and drift:

In that Reservation of quiet
The ferns gathered,
Changed, held their ground, and evolved.
Flowers weren't bothered.

Earth heaves over again.
Land masses clash
And rebound from each other.
Continents mash.

New sporelings wander the world –
Perch high in the trees,
Clothe banks, and float in the streams,
Colonize screes.

And Bracken rakes in his gold,
A great tycoon,
A subterranean emperor
Every June

Uncurling his gloved fists
Even against Grass –
A bit nouveau riche,
Just a bit brash!

But the *Dryopterids* (one of whose
Young fronds this is)
Keep the Fern's Way perhaps clearer
Than all of these.

They grow in the shade of woods,
By streams or rocks,
Tough-fronded, fibrous-rooting
With short blunt stocks.

They have lost the extravagant zest
Of the ancient trees.
You can't collect sackfuls of spores
Whenever you please!

They are modest things, friendly
In a fashion
And without great animosity
Or competitive passion.

John, don't be misled. They aren't us.
Tolerance is cheap.
They've no love for the animal kingdom.
They murder sheep.

They go out of their way to be useless.
They wear long hair.
They smoke hash in quakerish meetings.
They DO NOT CARE.

There's no hope in a fern, not a bit.
They've detachable sex.
Their spores are dehydrated lust –
Add water, and mix.

This poem was written in response to a poem by John Wain in 'Letters to Five Artists' (1969) about the fern in my back-yard. It was first published privately by Peter Hoy as part of my longer work, 'Visions and Praying Mantids: the Angelogical Notebooks' (Oxford, 1971.)

Sam Adams
Martins' Nest

In the old shed, high up, much magnified
And lit by sunlight gay with dust,
A martins' nest, like half an acorn cup

Or a clay blister plastered to the rafter.
And the parent birds gleaming in stippled
Rays like blue-black flames, then swallowed

Without trace in the scaled and roughcast cyst.
Despite the ladder's awkward stance, I climbed
Among rods of sun impelled through rusty pores

Rotted in the thin roof's corrugations,
Slanting pencil-thick to the oily floor,
Solid enough to my light-fingered touch.

Descending slowly to my upraised eyes
A crusted chalice growing from the beam;
Though my young feet fumble rungless spaces

My giant head rises by the lip.
In spontaneous combustion of feathers
The fledglings fled, their wingbeats scattering

Through the falling shed; I remember
The ladder reeling and my father's shout
Slicing the sunbeams before the light went out.

Graham Allen

A Scholarship

I knew it possible that streets stamped into place
night and morning by workmen's stiff boots
could change with a bit of chalk, a few kids' games,
another world lift out of the pavement.
Perhaps I even thought we lived under some such game,
in burrows tunnelled under the hollow roll of the coal trucks
and the slow cattle waggons breathing through dark slit sides
with secret jerkstrained eyes if I climbed close enough,
near the sky latticed and turning through the slow wheels;
how different the night-express with its yellow clatter
across the roofs and still bedrooms – like a memory
that only a drunken Saturday song could reach.
But real enough the final visit to the fitting-shop,
meal-time, and the men underfoot,
just torsos haunched on the floor between still lathes
the old fellow dumped before his work-tin,
his pint mug like a begging bowl waiting my rattle of news.

He wiped himself on a piece of waste, then congratulations
as we stood now, stiff-legged, stuck amid the grease-proof bits,
– shook hands as though he gave me leave to go
before I'd blurt out a new address,
as though I came to serve notice on him, and on home:
where we knew there was a table, set and neat,
where few called who didn't sit with us and eat.

Gillian Clarke
Lunchtime Lecture

And this, from the second or third millennium
B.C., a female, aged about twenty-two.
A white, fine skull, full up with darkness
As a shell with sea, drowned in the centuries.
Small, perfect. The cranium would fit the palm
Of a man's hand. Some plague or violence
Destroyed her, and her whiteness lay safe in a shroud
Of silence, undisturbed, unrained-on, dark
For four thousand years. Till a tractor in summer
Biting its way through the longcairn for supplies
Of stone, broke open the grave and let a crowd of light
Stare in at her, and she stared quietly back.

As I look at her I feel none of the shock
The farmer felt as, unprepared, he found her.
Here in the Museum, like death in hospital,
Reasons are given, labels, causes, catalogues.
The smell of death is done. Left, only her bone
Purity, the light and shade beauty that her man
Was denied sight of, the perfect edge of the place
Where the pieces join, with no mistakes, like boundaries.

She's a tree in winter, stripped white on a black sky,
Leafless formality, brow, bough in fine relief.

I, at some other season, illustrate the tree
Fleshed, with woman's hair and colours and the
rustling
Blood, the troubled mind that she has overthrown.
We stare at each other, dark into sightless
Dark, seeing only ourselves in the black pools,
Gulping the risen sea that booms in the shell.

John Tripp
In Memory of Idris Davies
(for Glyn Jones)

He was short and sturdy, one of dim Picton's Silurians –
dark, tough, stocky, thick-necked and durable,
bantam of a race that went down before the blonde Celts,
then packed the pits and Big Seats and choirs and scrums.
When you saw him in a drizzle on the Capitol steps
he wore a cloth cap, wool muffler, gloves and brown mac
with old wire specs askew, mended on wet-look solder,
one pebble-lens flattened tight to the eyeball.
He held his collier's Woodbine in the cup of his wounded hand,
easy and serene, without sulk or boiling mouth.

Rhymney and poverty made him. He was haunted to the very
end
by the skull of want and the furious gospel
lashed from the radical pulpits. Green dawns of childhood
by the river and black alp, dust-hung summer afternoons
among nettles in the pityard with the lost ragged boys
led him and them to the customary crawl
under the earth, along the seams of Gwent,
thin layer of grime washed off into the evening tub.
Then the long lonely track to shape himself,
the bitter chronicle beginning to itch inside his mind.

Out of such parched soil, such pitiless rock
his harsh plant grew. No document was ever carved before
from this slab of ferocity and love –
a wept lament for all those diggers in the dark
and their broken kin, abandoned in the tunnels of the south,
a testament of disgust drilled at the core of wrong.
He never served an image of moonlit brooks
or salmon-running streams, or blue remembered hills.
His was a bedded landscape of human figures
bent but proud before a random wind.

Memory must have plagued him like a pox
as his exiled heart was shuttled about England,
as honesty tested his acceptance
through the soft quilted ease of Bohemia.
In the staff-rooms of mouldering schools,
what remark could have triggered a vision
that shot him straight back to his bleakest ridge?
In those gay nights of bellowing talk,
did the turnkey suddenly slide in his greasy coat
to show him the ramshackle beauty of Wales?

Stripped, bare, stark and pure the lyrics come,
hard and lovely as the place that formed him,
true as the tribute to his ravaged land.
His goodness seeps down the years to remind us
of faith to be kept in the ruins. His last limp
over the mountain road, his suit hung loose on the frail bones,
will take him south again to the buttercup fields,
to the dream in the vale when he was young.
Your sad bells of Rhymney ring sweet and clear, Idris,
and the pigeons are homing. They are coming home.

Gillian Clarke
Burning Nettles

Where water springs, pools, waits
Collection in a bucket
In the late summer heat,
Beech trees observe foresight
Of autumn wrinkling their leaves.
The cold will wither this
Old garden. The plumpness shrinks
Beneath its skin, a light
Frown puckers the mirrored sky.

The scythe bleeds ancient herbs
Whose odours come as ghosts
To disturb memory,
My fire of nettles crackles
Like bees creeping in a green
Hive, making white smoke from weeds,
And the strange, sweet plants Marged
Sowed, or Nanu, before
The wind changed from the East.

With the reaping hook blade
I lift an exhausted moth
From the hot mound. It lives
To die of cold. Inside the cave
Of thatched grass the secret fire
Thrives on my summer. Nettles
Turn to ashes in its heart,
Crucible of the fragrant and
The sour; only soil survives.

Rose-bay-willowherb, ragwort,
Grass, disintegrate and make
A white continuous mane
For the mountain. Ponies turn

Windward. The evening's heat
Belies the beech trees' shiver,
And pinpoints of ice on skin
Are nettlestings, not rain. Fire
Buried in flower-heads, makes
Bright ritual of decay,
Transubstantiates the green
Leaf to fertility.

John Tripp
Dewi Emrys

Vagabond with a taste for wine and people,
he took four chairs and a crown,
then pawned the crown in Swansea for a couple of
                                    notes.
He slept under paper on the beggars' benches
and in Cardigan barns, glad of a crust of bread
or a ladle from the churn. On the street corners
through a screen of rain you might see him
hitch up his collar below the dripping troughs.

He should have been a cocky troubadour
stepping from tavern to tavern
with his slung lute, singing for his supper.
Our century could find no home for his heart.
What trouble takes a man of skill and vision
to the skidding edge? A wayfarer like all of us
but haunted, he journeyed from a warm centre
high in the bright pavilion of bards

to the lost shabby rim.
I think of him when he was alone
with only a pen and a gaping page,
facing an old language with humility,
testing the sounds, turning and turning the lines,
drumming their response through his head.

He sits with Dylan in that narrow room
where the lyric is measured, sealed and folded

into itself, where the craft is always stubborn.
I saw him once in a smoky distance
outside his nest at Talgarreg, sweeping the leaves.
He wore an old fisherman's hat and a leather jerkin,
seeming peaceful at last within that silent frame.
The moss is over him now, the briar and ivy.
His mark is a perfect quill and a brimming jug,
a short poem shaped like a heart.

Nigel Jenkins
Piglets

By morning she'd quartered the farrow,
tipped – by the flapping zinc or some stranger
in the yard – to a mother's lethal absolute.

The final pair, in too cool a huddle,
were eased from the arena of her jaw,
boxed in straw and shelved against the lagging
of our bathroom tank. Off school that day

with a cagey chest, I'd creak the boards
to see them (fed like me on whiskied milk)
twitch in frowning sleep. I scanned them once

at night, the torchlight glancing on a seam
of eye where, unfelt, a straw had lodged. The trees
outside cracked with cold as I sat
by my fire, singeing crayons on the bar.

Days later I found them, shrugged out
on the dunghill, skins coarse with frost,
decay postponed by protective weather.

Sheenagh Pugh
Thormod Kolbrunarskald
(died of wounds after the battle of Stiklestad, Norway, 1030.)

King's poet, war-poet, not one who spoke
of death at a distance, but one like Taliesin
who tasted it, who knew not only the word
for sword, but how it moves through air and bone.

Yet his friends did not call him battle-singer
but Kolbrun's poet. He was the man who made
love-songs to Kolbrun, the man who was a poet
for Kolbrun's sake. Where are now those songs?

There needs none, since he took her name with him
wherever he lived. Perhaps there were no songs,
only a man printing on all his actions
the name of Kolbrun, shaping into his poem

not the words for honour, endeavour, suffering,
but the things themselves, at last easing the arrow
from his wound with a graceful word, an artist always,
putting the final touch to Kolbrun's poem.

R.S. Thomas
Aberdaron

Here I think of the centuries,
six million of them, they say.
Yesterday a fine rain fell;
to-day the warmth has brought out the crowds.
After Christ, what? The molecules
are without redemption. My shadow
sunning itself upon this stone
remembers the lava. Zeus looked down
on a brave world, but there was
no love there; the architecture
of their temples was less permanent
than these waves. Plato, Aristotle,
all those who furrowed the calmness
of their foreheads are responsible
for the bomb. I am charmed here
by the serenity of the reflections
in the sea's mirror. It is a window
as well. What I need
now is a faith to enable me to outstare
the leering faces of the inmates of its asylum.

Nigel Jenkins
The Ridger

Capsized, by some nosing cow,
in the headland where last unhitched,
it raises to the solitudes
guide-arm, wing and wheel.

What should slide or spin
locks to the touch; a bolt-head
flakes like mud-slate at the push
of a thumb – fit for the scrapyard

or, prettified with roses, some
suburban lawn. Yet there persist,
in a tuck away from the weather,
pinheads of blue original paint.

To describe is to listen, to enter
into detail with this ground
and this ground's labour; to take
and offer outward continuing fruit.

My palm smooths the imperfect chill
of rusted iron... I weigh against
the free arm, easing up
the underside share – worms retire,
lice waggle away: it stands
on righted beam, rags of root-lace
draped from the delivered haft.

Maker and middleman emblazon
two cracked plaques: Ransomes, Ipswich;
White Bros., Pontardulais.
Less patent is the deeper tale
that gathers with the touch of rain
on the spike which was a handle,
the nail bent over for an axle-pin.

Christine Furnival
In the House of Bernarda Alba

I have glimpsed floral waterfalls of starwort
and rainbows of periwinkle, pimpernel and celandine –
but black lilies I'd never seen
till I entered the house of Bernarda Alba:
there are five tall black lilies
in the house of Bernarda Alba.

I've known fair skies go indigo, then black,
and then be turquoise once again;
and grey goose-feathered heavens
release pure white plumes to flurry and fall:
but a sky that had turned jet for once and all –
an ebon heaven I had never known
till I stood beneath the roof of the house of
      Bernarda Alba.
And took note that there even the sky was in hell.

And I've played, so help me, a number of games
with hearts I'd taken to be red,
and I've gambled with more than one black queen;
I've cursed those diamonds I should befriend,
I've stopped to pray for luck
at times when it was not fitting for prayers to be said.
– But government by one black heart
was a rule of play I'd never heard
till I entered the house of Bernarda Alba.
God help those trumped by such a ruthless card.

Legends I've heard of tornados
and of a still voice in a whirlwind;
and I have seen a great bridge
rock like a cradle in a gale.
Those winds that disjoin the mind
are to me no exception –
yet I'd never thoroughly known
storms that rush upwards from the planted roots
and have been harnessed from the moment of conception:
I dare swear such storms
trouble the soil beneath Bernarda's flowers
and must rape and snap all five stems in the end
of those five tall black lilies
in the house of Bernarda Alba.

(In the play by F.G. Lorca, the evil Bernarda Alba dominates and suffocates the lives of her five unmarried daughters.)

Chris Torrance
Carnival
(for Barry & Eve Pilcher)

Walking over the bodies of the dead
      at Llandaff
Ceremonial avenues, a clump of Scots pine
      on an island in the river
a jumble sale in Gabalfa
      A beckoning mound that
skimmed endlessly behind the horizon formed
by an advancing brow of larch
      as we rode gently along in the Morris Van

At least your pee looks good & green
in the white enamel bowl
A fit of the horrors
in a bar jammed with piratical scowls
& 5 o'clock shadows at noon
burnt grease stench ramming the air
riot talk thick & nauseous
haunted shagged faces of the night before
stare right down into the bottom of their beers

everyone looks like a murderer

PLATINUM STREET, ZINC STREET,
  PEARL STREET, TIN STREET,
    DIAMOND STREET, IRON STREET

"Cardiff was a dream"
as clear & lucid
as rays of sunlight
through a glass of pale ale
the pure Northerly tumbling
big awkward leaves of maple
towards the street of cardealers,
hands in pockets. The open-top Rambler

retailing at £395, the gas-gobbler
Dodge Coronet at £465
      a buyers market, plenty
of big fat bodies going
to the cruncher these days,
strip out all the items of use
then burn the sonofabitch
polluted smoke crowding the sky
turning out a box of
tightly compressed metal to be reintegrated
into the maw of the economic monster

METAL STREET, ORBIT STREET, BUTETOWN,
  GRANGETOWN, BESSEMER STREET
      Bessemer inventor of
      the convertor
turning pig iron to steel

tungsten carbide dumped
  behind rotted boards
    of torn Splottland deserts

the old dossers simmering over their
cider bottles below Hayes Island

TOPAZ STREET, LEAD STREET,
  RUBY STREET, EMERALD STREET,
    SAPPHIRE STREET, FOUR ELMS ROAD

  We pushed through the door into the
smoke of the Roath, where
grimy-necked men chatted & laught &
slapped each other

          the velvet bitter
slides down in thoughtful silence
creamy atomic mushroom explosions
trigger dead circuits into charging life, the talk begins

dreaming skulls nodding atop pineal spires

        the funny old dear
reading & rereading beermats with
shredded intensity   Weobley Castle, &
"a tradition as old
        as your next pint of Brains"

all tongues jerking ceaselessly frothing &
        foaming utterance
voiceroar blends into radiophonic mush
shiver exquisitely the orgasm drums,
the power drums, the dance of egos swarming
        the Roath Park a temple
        to the analgesic hop

COPPER STREET, STAR STREET, MOON STREET,
CONSTELLATION STREET, GOLD STREET,
SILVER STREET, METEOR STREET, PLANET
STREET,
COMET STREET, ECLIPSE STREET, THE
     ROYAL HAMADRYAD GENERAL &
     SEAMAN'S HOSPITAL

        *

& now in the morning
I sit here in the window
not quite sure whether I
have a hangover or not
sparrow perching on rosebud sends
dewdrops plummeting
how will today fill itself
with drops of life & death
the conundrum spouts distrails across the deep

Vernon Watkins
Prose

(All the pieces that follow were in Vernon's own hand) Excerpts from Vernon Watkins's lecture notes, used at University College, Swansea, in 1966

Style

IT HAS ALWAYS BEEN an axiom of mine that a true style cannot be learnt from a contemporary. I am not suggesting that poets living at the same time cannot help each other; they can do this, profoundly, but they cannot teach a style. Style is, I believe, a root thing, and roots do not run along the surface of letters. Although poetry is always, in one sense, revolutionary, because it takes the reader by surprise, it is always its relation to the past that gives depth. Since a poet is a witness, carrying news of his time to future generations, it would seem that the sharper and clearer his perceptions are, the more acute and lasting will be his findings; and yet, if clarity is the only criterion, his function will serve no better than a camera, and his art will be journalism. The perceptions of a poet must be composite, as he is a witness for the living and the dead at the same time. If he observes the two responsibilities, he will begin to see what is ancient in the contemporary scene and what is contemporary in the ancient; and his style will emerge from that collision, from that twofold perception. Only gradually does a poet find and begin to realize his particular task, for the task of each poet is different, and his true affinities in the poetry of past ages are not quickly understood. Style which has depth is recognised at once as it has immediacy, and also the corroboration of past ages; but among contemporaries it is distinction and opposition that foster style. True and different talents may feed each other, but they can only do so by obeying deep-rooted affinities, and by a divergence of style. The most fruitful relationship between contemporary poets is where a fundamental difference of style exists to serve a single truth, which then has more than one manifestation, or different truths which are bound together by affinity and indissoluble respect and affection.

If we look back through the centuries of our poetry we shall find many examples of these fruitful oppositions, of two poets innately and fundamentally different in idiom and style, but often bound by friendship and a common theme, whose work has been strengthened, not by competition, but by the assurance and expectation of works from a complementary talent. I think of Hopkins and Bridges, Browning and Landor, Shelley and Byron, Wordsworth and Coleridge, Shakespeare, Marlowe, and Ben Jonson, to name only a few; and European poetry is equally rich in these examples. Lyrically every poet is alone, but in the range of his development no poet is alone. Style is a root thing; development is something which unfolds.

Order and Luck

Criticism may assess, judge; but creation is never in a straight line. It follows what William Blake calls 'the crooked path of intuition'. The will, which is a daimonic thing, enables a poet to persist until he finds the right expression for this thought and matches the need of his imagination. The will is very important but alone it can do nothing, for the instinct of the will is to move in one direction, and creation is not in a straight line. So the will, always seeking a masterful understanding of the created world, is thrown back upon its own resources. I have seen a hawk, which was about to fall, caught up again into the clouds by the complexity of its own desire. The will of a poet is akin to this. It must operate with patience and great labour, and help him to reject all that does not exactly match his instinct for truth.

Protest and Gift

However complete a poet's equipment, he will achieve nothing that lasts without a gift. All he is able to do is to organise the argument of his poem, preparing it at each moment of pause for that possibility. Every pause is a test of conscience, and the poem proceeds with continual self-correction. In this discipline a poet can only really take credit for those efforts in which he fails, for the successful element in a poem always takes him by surprise, being a little beyond his powers, demanding them, like a magnet, but not completing his need until the gift itself does this. The need itself is the need either to state a vision or to resolve a thought which cannot be defined in prose; the verse-form contributes to his meaning, and an error of sound in verse will always be an error of meaning, a blurring of vision, or a confusion of thought.

Pity and War

David Jones's *In Parenthesis* is written in an idiom distinctively his own, but superficially bearing some resemblance to James Joyce's *Ulysses* and to Ezra Pound's *Cantos*. When Wilfred Owen first heard the sound of the guns in France he wrote a letter that it was 'a sound not without a certain sublimity'. Throughout *In Parenthesis* David Jones traces that sublimity through all the sordid and grotesque violence of war, with every kind of comic and tragic situation, and he resembles Owen in never losing sight of it. Never for a moment did David Jones lose sight of the heroes and victims of other wars either, and here he differs from Owen, who only occasionally refers to them. It is, as though, in the very heat of battle, those buried soldiers were as close to David Jones as the men at his side, even, sometimes, inhabiting their living or dead bodies. Yet, in description, there is sometimes a close resemblance to Owen, to Owen's late poem, 'Spring Offensive', for example.

Theory and Act

No permanent good in poetry can come from a restrictive theory of writing. The poet, or group of poets, equipped with such a theory, may issue a manifesto which will signpost a way of writing verse for a generation, and this will always prove a convenience to critics concerned with the prevailing movement of time. The perceptive critic must be on his guard, and his task is really to distinguish between theory and act. However intelligent a poet's theory may be, it does not bear fruit until the intervention of the creative act; the poem itself masquerades as its offspring, a kind of sandwich-man bearing the advertising boards. A true analysis of the poem will nearly always be in conflict with the theory it carries, for the struggle of a theory is one thing and the struggle of a poem another. The value of a theory lies only in its power to attack and purge but the value of the poem issues entirely from terms of peace. So far as the poem is concerned, the sandwich-man is advertising a campaign that is over.

Two sets of aphorisms
(note, 12.4.64)
1. When you find you are writing well, stop writing.
2. When critics praise you, don't believe them.
3. A poet's one currency is his reputation.
4. When you are writing badly, go on, and stick to your theme.
5. Don't let language jump the queue of your imagination.
6. An age labours; an instant co-ordinates.
7. Cold craftsmanship is the best container of fire.
8. When Dylan Thomas was struggling unsuccessfully with a theme he wrote to me: 'I am, in action, a person of words, and not, as I should be, a person of words in action.' This negative knowledge is necessary to the positive knowledge of what is true, when found.
9. Yeats said that a poem will suddenly fall into place, after long labour, like the click of a box. It is the conscious artificer who makes the box, the real artificer who clicks it.

Articulations, May 1955
A declared honesty is less valuable to an artist than an instinctive one.
That artist has no power who is not able to lay it down.
In art the real statements of power are those in which the whole intellect is involved, first in a suspension of power, and then in the renewal of power through grace.
To believe in a paradox is a half-truth; the whole truth is to live it as well.

Gwyn Williams
Under Orion – for D

Pissing under starlight I envy Orion's
bright erection as he now strides
over the dark humped warmth of Earth,

swinging across the sky to remind us
of the Boeotian hunter, killer of beasts,
one who at night's end lay in the bed

of dawn, made Eos blush, was killed
by Artemis, who wouldn't have him;
a mountain man who some say

was born of urine spirited on a bull's hide;
who now for us in frozen uprightness
pursues the sailing dove-girls in the moving

frieze of night's unaltering significances;
and as he still appears to veer
westwards away from Wales let me,

having sprayed this piece of mountain for my relief,
think of those things in my less violent life
which shamelessly make my emblem sparkling Orion,

who also took an eye of day to wife.

Tony Curtis
The Deerslayers
(A poem from the photographs of Les Krims)

Little guy coming out of your VW.
Pads so the ties don't mark your bonnet.
Taut across your roof the doe: her cleaned, gaping,
scraped belly is a door opening to the secret of all guts.

★

77

Stone-face of a movie G.I.
The door reveals you like some encapsulated wrong.
Wide-eyed, the buck draping your roof
testifies we use you for our killing.
*

Trunk of your Continental, a blanket folded under
the white-tailed doe as at a tame birth
(lanterns in the childhood barn).
Behind you, headlights screwing through the morning's
                                        haze to work.
*

Think Trout sticker on the window. Two deer
bleed open-mouthed over the roof edge. Check shirts,
jackets; giant camouflage footprints cover the camper.
Brautigan would approve such confusion, fusion.
*

You and your brother – such a likeness
into your 50's. Your grandson has the intense
determined look of a future lawyer.
Across the roof, that deer's white eye stretches to infinity.
*

A delta of blood from the leaking mouth
irrigates the dented wing.
Behind you, the land is ploughed and flat. No cover.
This buck's antlers close around you like claws.
*

Joker, face square alongside the strapped head
as you pose a nice-guy smile for the camera-flash.
It is evening: kneeling on the front seat your toddler
picks her nose and calls for bed.
*

You're out of the driver's window looking
back along the side to that head
spewing blood over the fender
of a Ford by Dietrich of Williamsville.
*

The bonnet of your Plymouth stretches like
a dirty pond in the flash-glare. Four of you

posed in the car. An extended radio aerial.
Over your heads an antlered head flies in the night.

*

Chevrolet NT 7729 from New York –
you are turning from the lens in protest.
Her hooves are safely wrapped in polythene.
Try to run: it is a wet morning and we have you on
                                                   record.

Philip Owens

Catechumens

The precisely-crossed hands
nervous for the tiny flake,
lips pursed for the silver cup's
rim, betray them.
                    The girls giggle
and the boys grin.
                    We've taken them
too young again. They will fall
before grasping that shimmering hem.

St Matthias' Day

Let us pray, says the priest,
for all estates of men:
in the words he gave say

Our Father... But the stain
of Akeldema spreads
about those who gather

the hard seed. The chosen
feel few in your red sun,
the mean harvest of creed.

For us all let us pray
with Judas at our backs,
upon whom the lot falls.

Raymond Garlick
An English Childhood

In the interminable raw
Pink roads with the sad bucolic
Names – Manor and Meadow and Close,
The ornamental cherry grows.

Exotic as the denizens,
It at least had established roots.
Life – in our square miles without church
Or pub – had left us in the lurch.

At school on Empire Day in May
Mixed Infants, Juniors, saluted
The flag, marched up and down on the wet
Yard. The sun had not begun to set.

My best friend and his mother drove
To mass on Sunday mornings, but
Each Sunday afternoon she'd spend
Marching with Mosley through the East End.

Chintzy and kind, a popular
Local councillor, she was
The typical suburban frau.
Where are all those English Blackshirts now?

They must be somewhere. There were so
Many of them, with their Union
Jacks and Nuremberg-rally drill.
I sometimes think I can hear them still.

Occasionally as a child
I too was taken up to London
By my mother or my aunt,
Believers in its power to enchant.

Unpaid footmen to the middle
Classes, stately policemen paced
The virtuous pavements of their beat,
Ushered one gravely across the street.

A rare treat that made your day
Was to go home able to say
You'd seen a coloured gentleman
Or better, a turbanned Indian.

Trooping the Colour; in the Mall
One day, holding my mother's hand:
'Who is that with the hearthrug-thing
Rolled up on his head?' 'Hush, it's the king.'

Thumping, clashing, blaring, the bands
Pounded inexplicably past:
'Who are that line of funny ones
Behind the king?' 'Hush, they're his sons.

They are the royal family.
Now you can say you've seen them all.'
'It doesn't look as though they enjoy
Being it.' 'Be quiet, you naughty boy.

What would your great-uncle Richard
Say? You know he's in the household.
You're very lucky to stand by
And see them all riding past.' 'But why?'

In Charing Cross Road with my aunt;
Men singing, begging by the kerb.
The crowd hurries past to avoid
Their cap. 'Welsh miners, unemployed.'

The Mall again, and chauffeurs serve
Champagne through the doors of waiting cars.
'We'll see the palace gates roll right
Back for them soon. There's a court tonight.'

The swastika flaps lazily
Above the German Embassy.
'Who lives there with the flag on top?
Uncle Richard?' 'Count von Ribbentrop.'

Such was my childhood in that strange
Barbaric country of the dead.
It was no Auden twitched my eyelid
To its meaning. Idris Davies did.

What makes me sad, who lived through it,
Is that you, for all your studies
Of Thirties poetry, your trim
Anthologies, never heard of him.

Jon Dressel
Cân Ryfelwr

A tough lot. You, the whole family.
After ten o'clock I steer clear
of you in the pub. You'd just as

soon have a punch-up as a short
at closing. I used to chalk it
just to your frustrations, your

bankruptcies, your dogged little
handyman enterprises that never
quite come off. Your daughters

leave school early and foal. Your
sons are not clever but are good
with their hands. Your wife pumps

petrol. Her arms are thick as yours.
The woodwork on your council house
goes blistered and bare. You work

elsewhere. They say you were
fierce at rugby once. Monoglot
English from birth, you were all

I despaired of in the future of Wales.
You were the gwerin, beaten thin
at last, sullen, unremembering, nothing

but a bloke. Then I saw you this morning,
in a field with a standing stone
at the edge of the village. You had

a red horse, in the early sun,
and you raced it round and round
you in what seemed a great clean circle

of the flesh made blaze, its head high,
your eyes raised, intent, as though
you held it by your gaze more than

the long thin lead. You hardly moved.
You turned like stone. It was
just work, yet something more essential

than the stress of small contracting
put the pressure on your blood.
You wheeled the taut red horse like fire,

that whole half hour. It was your work,
yet tired land rose, the land had force,
the clean horse came, the sunned stone sang.

Christopher O'Neill
Dichtung und Wahrheit

Language – you old Mediterranean
Tideless and rich in oily flotsam
Of unplumbed and unutterable emotion –
You have learned to move me from inside.

We collaborate: like an aging Pavlov
You intend my response, say 'grove'
Where I might have said 'trees', 'love'
When I might have said: the dyed

Blue shades of the wallpaper depth –
Charge my seaweed inept
Submarine searchings for the root of 'be'.
And it's all too much: the calm swell
Chokes up inside my hollow shell,
And the wages of feeling is apathy.

John Tripp
Zeal of the Convert

Bluebottles dive and buzz
against a porthole in The Trappist Arms.
When somebody moves, a mongrel
growls from the mat. I order a pint
in English. 'Don't speak that heathen
tongue here,' he says, the one just come

from a Saxon campus. He is not
joking. (For an instant the terrible image
blazes, as I see myself catapulted
out of a culture.) Then I lift two fingers
in the dismissive V, and wonder:
If we were dumb, would we be less Welsh?

White Flag

The climate kept me indoors
remembering more reckless days.
Soon my typing quarto had gone
so I used the backs of bills;
only one biro functioned
then the dictionary fell apart.
Ideas dissolved in my notebook.

('Keep going' they wrote. 'Don't quit
now. Salvage something from the wreck.
This country isn't finished yet.'
All right for them, in their mountain
fastnesses, untouched by southern blight.)

As doubt dribbled down to sloth
and the toast burnt, the soup boiled over,
I thought it was time to stop.
Dreams had kept me bolt upright for years.
On a bitter Monday morning in March
the fire went out in my belly.
Outnumbered, I surrendered with bad grace.

Dannie Abse
Last Words

Splendidly, Shakespeare's heroes,
Shakespeare's heroines, once the spotlight's on
enact every night, with such grace, their verbose deaths.
Then great plush curtains, then smiling resurrection
to applause – and never their good looks gone.

The last recorded words too
of real kings, real queens, all the famous dead,
are but pithy pretences, quotable fictions
composed by anonymous men decades later,
never with ready notebooks at the bed.

Most do not know who they are
when they die or where they are, country or town,
nor which hand on their brow. Some clapped-out actor may
imagine distant clapping, bow, but no real queen
will sigh, 'Give me my robe, put on my crown.'

Death scenes not life-enhancing,
death scenes not beautiful nor with breeding;
yet bravo Sidney Carton, bravo Duc de Chavost
who euphoric, beside the guillotine, turned down
the corner of the page he was reading.

And how would I wish to go?
Not as in opera – that would offend –
nor like a blue-eyed cowboy shot and short of words,
but finger-tapping still our private morse, '...love you,'
before the last flowers and flies descend.

Tony Curtis
The Freezer

When they finally broke in
the place smelled like Pompeii –
dust like ash, fall-out inches thick.
She was sitting there, a queen propped
up in bed and not looking so hot.

In the garage an A.C.
road racer from the '30s worth thousands –
quality coachwork under the dust, and not a scratch.

All types of fungi in the kitchen,
but the freezer was stocked and neat –
twenty-nine stiff cats packed and labelled:
'Roland' – 'Katherine' – 'Veronique' –
and so on, reading like a list of social
acquaintances. Curled, stretched, flat or sprung,
as if the shape gave each one a character.

The next evening, mackerel-eyed, fur
stuck like old pasting brushes,
they got shovelled into the garden.

The green eye of the freezer glowed,
the frosted chest purred and shuddered
in the empty house
until they cut off the mains.

Mike Jenkins
Laughter Tangled in Thorn

Dressed like a child
for our ritual Sunday afternoon
pilgrimage to the hillside:
your pear-shaped hood,
scarf wound like a snake
and red ski-boots dragged along
like grown-up things worn for a dare.

When I laugh, I don't mean it to hurt.
It is the brother of the laugh
at the end of our love-making –
rigid bones melting into blood.

The moor grass has turned
into a frosty yellow, its green
gone deep into hibernation.
We crunch mud, step streams,
in games which strip us of years
like the trees have been
of their leaves. The water
and your green eyes
share the only motion.

You see a red berry
and call it a ladybird.
I think of your city upbringing;
the seasons being passing strangers
through Belfast streets
where you cadged rides from the ice.

When the brook's chatter is snow-fed,
your laughter is tangled in thorn.
You discover an ice sculpture
mounted on a spine of reed,

and call it 'Teeth and Jaws'.
The light of your words
travels through it.

High above Merthyr, mountain lapping mountain,
you are amazed at the rarified sunlight!
When you speak, the numb streets
are startled. We leave the childhood
of the moorland, to grow taller
with a tiredness which is the sister
of when we lie, translucent and still,
on the single spine of our bed.

Anne Stevenson
Letter to the Editor

22 Broad Street,
Hay-on-Wye.

DEAR CARY ARCHARD

You ask for an 'impression' of Wales. How does an American feel about living here? Why did we move to Wales from Oxford? The answer has to be that we didn't know, when we started The Poetry Bookshop, that Hay was in Wales. When in doubt (as the bones of every American say) move west. West to us was Herefordshire where Michael hoped to find a job on the fringes of agriculture – in a feed mill or in poultry research. (We have, in fact, been asked locally to supply information about our "poultry bookshop"!) But while Michael was reconnoitering in Hereford, I spoke to Robin Waterfield, founder of the famous antiquarian bookshop in Oxford, who suggested that we start our own bookshop in Hay, with his assistance. As it turned out, a grant from the Arts Council and a legacy from my father gave us (an

American prerequisite) 'the hard cash of opportunity.' We set up in business – if business is what we do here – in the laundry of the old town workhouse which we were able to rent for very little money from Richard Booth.

Around Christmas time in 1979, we moved the bookshop from Booth's premises in Frank Lewis House to our own house at 22 Broad Street. Since both Michael and I want time to write more than we want a vast profit, and since we are both unhappy in cities and fond of the country, Hay – rather than Wales – seemed an ideal place to live. In most ways, though, Hay is not Wales but as independent a town as Richard Booth has proclaimed it to be. With his castle in ruins and his empire threatened by such bureaucratic monsters as The Welsh Tourist Board, King Richard continues to manufacture Hay passports and sweatshirts bearing the legend "Balls to Walls. Eat Hay National Ice Cream" for the entertainment of his customers. All romp and circumstance, he parades in crown and robes on Independence Day (April 1st), hurling indictments and mockery at imaginary enemies.

But the independence of Hay is really proclaimed in more subtle ways. Most of the people who have lived here for a long time – as opposed to those who moved here in some gesture of escape from urban megalopolis – are either Welsh (the trades-people, the town councillors, most of the builders and tenant farmers, the smallholders) or border-upper-class English who traditionally have been Herefordshire landowners. There is, of course, a smattering of retired people – army officers, businessmen, teachers – as there are a number of artists and craftsmen, who have buried themselves in the hills for privacy. But these fit easily enough into the mixture, as do the confirmed eccentrics of independent soul and means, who are wedded to country life and muddy landscapes as old soldiers are wedded to the army.

For a town which supports fourteen independent bookshops, two art galleries, several crafts centres, a number of antique shops as well as some excellent restaurants and pubs, Hay is a surprisingly quiet, unselfconscious, unaffected, egalitarian place with a cattle market on Mondays (pubs open all day) and a stall market on Thursdays (pubs open all day), conservative in outlook without being antagonistic to new-comers. Indeed, endemic conservatism suits both the royalist assumptions of the English and the small-town suspicions of the native Welsh, resident prejudices getting on well where there are no students or 'intellectuals' to stir up class warfare. Richard Booth and the 'court' he rather imposed on Hay are tolerated, even where they are disliked. The prevailing philosophy seems to be 'Everyone to his own thing, and if they make money at it, so much the better.' There is really no cultural life in Hay, though any number of highly educated 'cultured' people live here, having limped this far after disastrous encounters with the great world.

How, you ask, can such a *laisser-faire*, commercial atmosphere be conducive to the writing of poetry? Where are your fellow poets? Where is there a theatre, a concert hall? (The nearest cinema which is not filled with second-hand books is in the Arts Centre in Builth Wells.) And what a distortion of the real state of society – in industrial South Wales, in Birmingham – must life in Hay represent! How can you write honestly of late 20th century in a country backwater, no matter how beautiful the landscape?

The answer must be a personal one, as all such answers are. I suppose that for me (and for Michael, who does all the real work of the bookshop) Hay is a microcosm of the human community which is still knowable, understandable, at first hand. The horrors of a mass society are not in evidence here, but the strengths and weaknesses of human beings are everywhere observable. Hay is the ideal size for a town – for what sociologists might call a 'human living unit'. It is large enough for essential privacy (you can do anything you want, even write poetry, so long as it doesn't interfere with anyone else) but small enough to give each inhabitant an essential importance. In the post office, in the food shops, you nod to familiar faces. You know your butcher (he lived across the street), your neighbours, your tobacconist, the couple who run 'The Blue Boar', the ladies in the fish shop, the ladies in the pet shop. Everybody has a dog, and you know who goes with which dog. And not only do you know these people, you care about them. No one is a statistic, not even the lady who comes to measure up your house for the rates assessment. There is an unspoken assumption – as there is in any small community – that somehow we are all in it together. This being the case, no amount of wealth or talent or power seems especially impressive. We sell books and write poetry. Our next door neighbour is a printer. Next to the printer, good friends of ours sell antique pianos. Another friend, a fine classicist, has just made a harpsichord there; in a few weeks it will be played in concert.

And all this activity goes on without fanfare. Art becomes amateur in the root sense of that word when whatever is made, be it music, food, beer, poetry, is made for the needful love of it, not without an eye for its worth, but patently without the taint of a personal ambition for glory.

There is much of the world – of Wales – that we miss in Hay. In a sense it's an escapist's haven. On the other hand, is it not better to live poorly but as one believes, in an inconspicuous and nourishing community instead of fighting megalopolis, mass behaviour, personality cults in the withering conditions of computerized agony and mass make-believe gloss? If Wales is still Wales and not part of an endless economic suburb of New York and London, then it is worth fighting for, community by community, town by town.

Poverty is degrading, and there is unforgivable poverty in the Welsh valleys. But it seems to me more degrading still to sell the soul of a community for the sake of mythical European unity, for a featureless urban sprawl in which only a few people will be able to crawl to the top of the rat race, through a policy of agreeing to be rats.

If I were Welsh I would be a Welsh Nationalist – a small-community-regional-nationalist. As it is, I feel like an American faced with the frontier of an unexplored country. Richard Booth may be on the right track after all. Hay for Hay. Wales for Wales. And to hell with the standardizing, centralizing, economic bulldozers politicians like to call progress.

Yours sincerely,
Anne Stevenson

Joseph P. Clancy
from The Sound of the Wind that is Blowing

(A translation of 'Swn y Gwynt Sy'n Chwythu' by J Kitchener Davies)

Today,
there came a breeze thin as the needle of a syringe,
cold, like ether-meth on the skin,
to whistle round the other side of the hedge.
For a moment, I felt a numbness in my ego,
like the numbness of frost on the fingers of a child
climbing the stiles of Y Dildre and Y Derlwyn to school;
only for a moment, and then the blood flowed again,
causing a burning pain such as follows numbness on fingers,
or ether-meth on the skin after the first shiver.
      It did not come through the hedge
though I could recognize its sound blowing,
and feel on my face
the foul breath of graves.
But the hedge is thick-trunked, and high,
and its shelter firm so that nothing comes through it,
– nothing at all but the sound of the wind that is blowing.

★ ★ ★

You went down to Tonypandy for the Strike and the
                              General Strike,
for the jazz carnival, and the football of strikers and police,
to the soup-kitchens and the cobbling,
the jumble-sales for sore-ridden Lazarus,
helping to sweep the spare crumbs from the boards for the
dogs under the tables,
pouring alms like rubble on the tips
or sowing basic slag on allotment gardens of ashes
to cheat the arid earth into synthetic fertility.

      There the hedges had fallen and the gaps were gaping
and the narrow streets were like funnels for the whirlwind's
pouring, blast upon blast,

93

to whip the corners and raise the house-tops
whirling wretches like empty chip-bags
from wall to post, from gutter to gutter;
the cloudbursts and the hailstones choking every grating
splitting the pavements and flooding through the houses,
and clanging like a death-rattle in the windowless cellars;
and famine like a stiff broom sweeping through the homes
from front to back and over the steep garden-steps,
down the back-lane to the river's floods, –
the wrack and black water pouring from the valley
to be battered and spewed to the level land's hollow banks,
rubbish abandoned to rot.

    And there you were like Canute on the shore,
or like Atlas in a coal pit
with your shoulder under the rocks holding back a fall,
or with your arms outstretched between the crag and the sea
shouting 'Hey! Hey!'
in the path of the crazed Gadarene swine.

    O yes, you challenged the whirlwind's teeth
and climbed to the top of the tree bent in half
by the tempest's shocks, until you needed
to sink your nails in the bark and close your eyes
to keep from becoming drunk with the sway of your mast.

    Remember,

there was no need for you, more than the rest of your fellows,
to scream your guts out on a soap-box
on the street-corners and the town-squares:
that was the sort of thing expected in a muffler-and-cap,
not nice in a collar-and-tie.
No call for you to march in the ranks of the jobless,
your dragon-rampant hobnobbing with the hammer-and-
                                   sickle,
up to the square of Y Petrys, down Ynyscynon and across Y
                                   Brithweunydd,

past y Llethr-ddu to y Porth and y Ddinas
and back over Tylacelyn and through Coed y Meibion
to the field of Y Sgŵar, and the waggons, the megaphone,
                    the open-mouthed thousands.

★ ★ ★

No!
there was no need for you
to dare the Empire and the Hippodrome packed on Sunday
                    evening,
– you a dandy bantam on the dung-heap of the spurred cocks
of the Federation and the Exchange –
but you ventured,
and ventured in elections for the town Council and the County
and Parliament presently
against Goliath in a day that knows no miracle, –
the giant with picks of posts as a sweetener on your bread,
while you reached out your slice and begged like a clever
                    slave.
Well no, I am not ashamed to admit
that the garden near the house has been turned over through
                    the years
and diligently weeded, till the back was near breaking;
but the soil is stronger than I, the convolvulus
like cancer twisting itself through the bowels
squeezing life to the ground, inch by relentless inch.
The deeper I dug, the swifter would wind
the snake-like convolvulus through the loose soil,
climbing each stake and bush beneath my hands
and strangling the roses and the beans in their flowering
and raising their pure white bells like banners,
or like girls with petal-like lips
baring their teeth to smile whitely
with no laughter reaching their eyes, nothing but rancour in
                    those pools.
I wanted to save Cwm Rhondda for the nation
  and the nation itself as a garden that had fertility.

'How often I desired to gather your chicks but you did not
desire it.'
But it was a boost to the heart to hear passers-by over the
garden wall
begging me – 'Stop killing yourself, simpleton;
you're working too hard from morning to evening,
from spring to autumn, and your garden's soil will not pay
you.'
Then as they turned to their strolling I heard:
'There he is, doubled over, so foolish, so foolish.'
And the furtive weeds stealing bed after bed
so that only a single bed was clear of their ravening,
my home, my wife, and three little lasses, –
Welsh-speaking Welsh and proud as princesses.
Yes, I confess that I tried to hurl myself
into the whirlwind's teeth to be raised on its wings
and be blown by its thrust where it willed
as a hero to save my land.
Since it not only blows where it will, the tempest,
but blows what it will before it where it will;
'Who at its birth knows its growth,' I said.

* * *

John Tripp
Louis MacNeice in the 'Cock'

Great Portland Street at opening time, at dusk
when the jewellers and rag-traders locked up
and the broadcasters filed to their booze.
He was there most nights when the Third
didn't stick his brilliance in a cubicle
with knobs, buttons, switches and dials
waiting for a red light to flick.
On summer afternoons he watched cricket at Lord's.

Everything about him was dark:
he wore a black leather coat
standing alone at the bar
like a rich romantic French actor
or a matador taking his ease.
I hoped Auden would come in from New York
to break his silence, making
a double flash of glamour
among the clerks and tartan panels.

I never approached him, being nothing much
at the Old Beeb, and he
seemed formidable, with a known flair
for testiness, and a cold-blooded gift
for disdain – leaning back, holding a glass
and looking at the world from a distance
through half-closed eyes. It was an aloof
hooded glance, to keep people away
and his distinction intact. It was what
Spender called a superior head
with lancing eyes sizing you up.
I thought then he did not belong,
that somehow he would not grow old.

He was *in* life, yet above it –
a shocked observer pretending to be amused.
In the Cock Tavern long ago
his *Autumn Journal* was inside his head
and his eyes seemed fixed on some débâcle:
'Crumbling between the fingers, under the feet,
Crumbling behind the eyes,
Their world gives way and dies
And something twangs and breaks at the end of the
                                                street'.

Thomas Dilworth
In Parenthesis as Chronicle

I asked David Jones, 'What do you think of Yeats?'
'Not much,' he replied.
'What don't you like about him?'
'Hard to say, exactly, but there's something missing.'
'What do you mean?'
'Oh, the Plato-Aristotle thing.'

IN PARENTHESIS DERIVES from David Jones's experience as a private soldier in the trenches during the seven months of the Great War that culminated in the Battle of the Somme. Jones chronicles his experience, and examines it in its relation to the traditions of Western culture. Through allusions to history, literature, scripture, liturgy, and folklore, Jones provides correlatives to the experience of modern war, and tests the validity of traditional values. Jones's literary and existential purpose naturally influences the character of his chronicle. For him war is myth in action, but so is life, and the two are basically the same myth. He implies this when he says that *In Parenthesis* has its title because 'the war itself was a parenthesis... and also because our curious type of existence here is altogether in parenthesis'[1]. The disclosure of war's mythic pattern, and therefore of its relation to the whole of human experience, requires emotional objectivity missing in much of the literature written by other combatants. Emotional objectivity is only possible for Jones because he begins to write almost a decade after the end of the war. But objectivity does not come to those who merely wait, it is a technical achievement involving decisions about content and tone.

As chronicle, *In Parenthesis* is generally historically accurate. Jones's battalion of Royal Welch Fusiliers (London Welsh) marched from Winnal Down through Southampton, and then embarked on the fifth of December 1915 to Le Havre. The next day they arrived at Warne and, after two weeks of further training, they marched toward the trenches, resting on the way at Reiz Bailleul. The dates and place-names are not given in the poem, but this is its exact sequence and setting to the end of Part 3. Jones spent part of Christmas day on fatigue duty behind the lines, just as the poem's central figure, John Ball, does in Part 4 on Christmas Day[2]. The poem's Part 5 telescopes actual events of the spring: the first, ominous, issuing of metal shrapnel helmets (104); the 'quite successful raid' (106); the general alert during an unsuccessful German offensive (108); the outdoor concert, at which a corporal really did sing 'Thora' (110); the march south to the Somme; and an officer's reading of the 'good news' of initial British success (123) – this took place on July first, and the infantrymen actually were 'permitted to cheer'[3]. Then in Part 6 is the confused marching which robbed the battalion of sleep and brought it to battle exhausted. In Part 7 is the assault on Mametz Wood on July tenth, commencing at 4.15 a.m.; the digging of the trench that afternoon at map coordinates 'V, Y, O & K' (172) – you can still see this shallow trench in the wood today; and finally the wounding of Private David Jones, reflected in the wounding of the poem's John Ball, shortly after midnight on the eleventh. Throughout the narrative, dates and place-names are generally withheld – Mametz Woods is always, for example, simply 'the wood' – so that the narrative is at once intimate and universal in a way that conventional documentary reporting cannot be.

There are only two important changes in chronology. Jones's battalion first entered trenches on the night of December nineteen. In the poem, this is moved forward to Christmas Eve, so that the first day in trenches is Christmas. The change compresses the action and better accommodates the poem's seasonal and liturgical imagery. The other important change occurs near the end of the poem on the afternoon before the assault. John Ball and some friends watch waves of infantry going forward to attack what must be Mametz Wood, and they

wondered for each long stretched line going so leisurely down the slope
and up again, strained eyes to catch last glimpses where the creeping
smoke-screen gathered each orderly
deployment within itself. (150)

The terrain is right. To reach the wood the assault-force had to cross over 500 yards of no-man's land which dropped steeply fifty feet into a valley and then rose for 400 yards to the edge of the wood[4]. But the time is wrong. The wood was not under attack on the ninth. It had last been assaulted, unsuccessfully, on the seventh, when Jones was not in the vicinity to observe. But he did see what he describes[5]. And the only time he could have seen it was on the morning of the tenth, just before joining in the assault and himself becoming part of the picture he gives us. In the poem, Jones moves the description to the previous afternoon where it becomes an objectively perceived image of things to come, and where it affords no visual or emotional relief from the next morning's myopic awareness and increasing anxiety in the moments immediately before battle. Jones had seen the 16th Royal Welch Fusiliers advancing, before his own battalion left the shelter of Queen's Nullah. In the poem, the action is condensed and there is no delay: Ball's battalion goes over the top with the first assault troops. Such changes in chronology indicate that Jones is not recording history, but he is being over careful when he writes in his preface that no 'sequence of events' in the poem is 'historically accurate' (ix).

Jones also writes that 'none of the characters in this writing are real persons' (ix), and this too might be misleading. The narrative is fictionalized. Jones's 15th Battalion becomes the imaginary 55th. With only a few exceptions, moreover, characters are not called by their actual names[6]. Throughout almost all of the poem, for example, John Ball stands in for David Jones. Ball has Jones's experiences and, like Jones, Ball is clumsy, 'a parade's despair' (xv). After Ball, the poem's important narrative reflectors are Private Aneirin Lewis and Lieutenant Piers Dorian Isambard Jenkins. Together they combine to epitomize the battalion's dual Welsh-and-English character. I once asked Jones whether Aneirin Lewis, with his thorough knowledge of Welsh tradition, is a real person. 'Yes,' said Jones, 'as with other characters, a combination of people: he may have been Aneirin Evans and Cadwaladr Lewis.' Likewise, Lt. Jenkins represents a combination of prototypes.

In a letter to Colin Hughes, Jones writes that one prototype was 'an attractive man, very absent minded, and also fair-haired like the squire for the Rout of San Romano' to whom he is likened in the poem, but without "the 'elegance' intended to be implied by my choice of the names Piers, Dorian, Isambard."[7] The prototype of Jenkins is also the prototype of Talbot Rhys, who is Jenkins's friend in the poem, and who is killed in the raid in Part 5. The raid corresponds to an actual raid in which the prototype of Rhys and of Jenkins actually was killed. The other model for Jenkins is an officer who fell during the assault immediately in front of Jones soon after leaving the assault trench and not, like Jenkins in the poem, close to the edge of the wood[8]. Other figures, like Colonel Dell, 'Aunty Bembridge', and Signaller Olivier, are based on single prototypes whose names alone have been changed.

The narrative of *In Parenthesis* is basically chronicle, but without the conventional restrictions of documentary reporting that govern point of view and diminish sensory imagery. In this regard, the poem anticipates modern documentary fiction. But *In Parenthesis* is even more radically fictionalized. It involves a greater freedom about what to include in the narrative and what to exclude. And always the choice is a matter of technique.

Jones excludes anecdotes. He himself was an inveterate teller of war stories. He used to tell, for example, how his colonel – J. C. Bell, the prototype of the poem's Colonel Dell – after hearing that Jones was 'educated', repeatedly urged him to become an officer. 'I kept declining,' Jones said.

Officers in their boots and close-cut coats had different silhouettes and were easy for the enemy to distinguish and aim at. He said I was shirking my duty. When finally I told him I had gone to *art* school, he dropped the subject.

Once Dell caught Private Jones carrying on his back half a barn door which he had taken from a farmhouse:

As I went, the door got heavier and I got more bent over. Suddenly I saw a pair of spotless boots. 'What are you doing with that door?' 'I'm going to make a fire with it, sir.' 'We pay rent to the French.' It's true, we did pay rent, for the trenches. 'I'm not saying your regiment isn't brave,' he said, enjoying himself very much, 'but you've got a bad reputation for *stealing*! Take it back where you got it.' I did, and found some sticks somewhere instead. The next day the house was blown to buggery.

This may be the farmhouse whose destruction is foretold on the poem's page ninety-six, but the personal anecdote is not recorded. And there are other anecdotes: about Lazarus Black, the prototype of the poem's 'little Jew' (155); about finicky and stupid General Price-Davies, the prototype of Aunty Bembridge; and about a night raiding party Jones was part of, whose members suffered an attack of nervous giggling within a few feet of an occupied German trench[9]. Nothing like any of this gets into the poem. Such miniature dramas would distract from the larger pattern. You cannot plant little plots in a work that has no plot without those little plots dominating the whole. And as a whole, the narrative is plotless. Infantrymen are 'pawns' (165), they suffer; they do not initiate or control action.

Anecdotes also round out character, and Jones wants his characters flat. He identifies them with single traits. Aneirin Lewis remembers, Lte. Jenkins daydreams, John Ball is clumsy. They could be almost anybody, and Ball as the central figure is a sort of archetypal Anybody. Because flat characters do not engage or compete with the reader's ego, they free the reader from personality. Consequently they are better than round characters would be at mediating the work's symbolic dimensions.

Although Jones shuns anecdotes, autobiography does inform the narrative. Always, however, the meaning is never merely personal, and usually it has a symbolic dimension. For example, at the end of Part 2 Jones's fictional proxy, John Ball, experiences a shell-explosion in vivid slow motion. It is a 'Pandoran' epiphany of 'all unmaking' (24). Jones told me he actually experienced this explosion as Ball does in the poem. Like Ball, he had just given matches to a lieutenant whom he had failed to address properly as 'sir'. So the ironic contrast between a breach of etiquette and a breach in ontology is remembered, not invented. And after the explosion, the blood-red sap of mangolds really did slobber 'the spotless breech-block' of a nearby artillery piece.

Similarly, on Christmas morning Germans sing the carol 'Es is ein' Ros' entsprungen' and the British irreverently counter with 'Casey Jones' (67-68). In the poem, this exchange becomes an ironic pastoral song-contest, which heightens the morning's violation of the conventions of classical and Christian pastoralism. But Jones said that on Christmas morning, 1915, the Germans really did sing that carol and the British really did try to drown it out with 'Casey Jones'.

And on the eve of the assault, Jones, like Ball, heard hammering 'as though they builded some scaffold for a hanging' (154). Actually they were building coffins but, Jones said, 'Ball didn't know what was being made,' and we may assume that neither, at the time, did Jones. The poem's symbolism moves from scaffold to gallows-cross to Calvary ('the place of the skull'(154), but the movement begins in something actually heard.

The meaning of a memory partly determines whether it is included in the narrative. But the overriding criterion governing selection is tone, which is the relationship of narrative consciousness to narrated event. Jones consistently ensures that this relationship is immediate, sometimes at the expense of broad historical perspective. A recovery of this perspective makes possible an appraisal of this aspect of Jones's narrative technique.

Artillery fire lasts the length of the poem's Part 6. Jones must have known when writing the poem that this was, to date, the greatest artillery bombardment in military history. He may have been tempted to say so. He does write that the Somme is 'the magnetic South' (119), which implies that it attracts all available canon and shells. There was, in fact, one howitzer or mortar for every seventeen yards of enemy front line – 1,437 big guns to fire almost two million shells during the barrage that began on June twenty-fourth and could be heard as far away as the coast of England[10]. Everywhere in the background of Part 6 is artillery fire, but that is where it stays, in the background. The poem's infantrymen know no more than infantrymen then knew: unending noise and the night sky on fire. Jones rejects the historical perspective which might have enriched his chronicle, but which would have placed the reader's view outside that of the infantrymen.

Sometimes Jones excludes irony along with historical perspective. When writing the poem, he knew that the raid in which Talbot Rhys dies was, according to General Headquarters' dispatches, 'the third best raid carried out so far by the British Army'[11]. But to have said so would have been to relinquish the immediate awareness of a private soldier for the perspective of the officers who evaluated the raid and sent the dispatches. Instead, Jones simply writes, 'The raid had been quite successful' (106), so that the irony is not heavy-handed when it comes: 'Mr Rhys and the new sergeant were left on his [the enemy's] wire; you could see them plainly, hung like rag-merchants' stock' (106). Immediacy mitigates irony.

Another decision for immediacy over historical perspective and ironic effect involves the waves of men walking 'so leisurely' (150) towards Mametz Wood. The usual and much safer tactic was (and still is) to assault in short rushes between cover[12]. But on July tenth, the infantry walked slowly in 'admirable formation, in the high-port position' (162), four paces between each man, 100 yards between each line of men. This carefully rehearsed slow walk was especially invented for the Battle of the Somme by General Henry Rawlinson, who believed the new recruits of his Fourth Army would not otherwise keep ranks in a frontal attack on strongly fortified enemy positions. And so line after long line of infantrymen walked slowly into the devastating fire of enemy machine guns. They were, in fact, forbidden to run until within twenty yards of enemy trenches. The Germans, seeing them coming, thought them mad[13]. The number of British casualties was high, as Jones suggests: one-third of Ball's section reaches the Wood, and of his platoon of sixty, only nineteen. But Jones does not inform us in the poem or in its notes that the lines of walking men are disciplined against their own safety on this occasion only and by their own commanding officer. If Jones had told us this, he would have generated a bitter irony and gained historical perspective, but at the expense of narrative immediacy and narrative consistency. The universal character of the experience of assault would have been lost, furthermore, in a particularized historical moment.

In Parenthesis is one of the world's four or five great war books. It is far better than any other work or collection of works on the Great War. The importance of *In Parenthesis* as a work of literature does not lie in its documentary aspect, but it does begin there, for even as a war record, *In Parenthesis* is a model of technique. As chronicle it maintains an objectivity to match that of the work's multi-layered allusions. It also achieves an immediacy that allows easy movement between sensory experience and the interior matrix of the allusions by which modern war becomes an epiphany of "our curious type of existence here." In these allusions, but perhaps more clearly in the underlying chronicle, Jones bases his aesthesis on the Aristotelean reality-principle, and in a way that demonstrates both the limitations and the validity of his favourite words of Picasso, that the artist 'does not seek, he finds'.

NOTES

1 *In Parenthesis* (London: Faber and Faber, 1969), p. xv. Page references to this text appear hereafter in parenthesis.

2 See David Jones, *The Anathemata* (New York: Viking, 1955), p. 216.

3 Rene Hague, *Dai Greatcoat* (London: Faber and Faber, 1980), p. 72.
   Except where otherwise noted, my bases for determining the historical accuracy of Jones's narrative are Llewelyn Wyn Griffith, *Up to Mametz* (London: Faber and Faber, 1920), and *A History of the 38th (Welsh) Division* by the G.S.O.s I of the Division, Lieut. Colonel. E. Munby, ed. (London: H. Rees, Ltd, 1920).

4 Wilfred Miles, *History of the Great War, Military Operations, France and Belgium, 1916* (London: Macmillan, 1938), pp. 49-53.

5 The authors of *A History of the 38th (Welsh) Division* record that 'one of the most magnificent sights of the war' was 'wave after wave of men... advancing without hesitation and without a break', and Jones notes in the margin of his copy of this book, 'I saw something of this myself and it was an impressive sight'. For a complete transcription of Jones's marginalia in his copy of the book, see my article, 'A Book to Remember by:

David Jones's Glosses on a History of the Great War', *The Papers of the Bibliographical Society of America 74* (1980), 221-234.

6 The exceptions are 'Reggie with the Lewis-Gunners' (74), who is Reggie Allen, the 'PTE. R.A. LEWIS – GUNNER' of the poem's dedication; 'Elias the Captain' (136), who is Captain Thomas Elias; and ''79 Jones' (108). David Jones once told me, 'There were three Jones in my regiment. I was '79 Jones'.

7 Colin Hughes, *David Jones: the Man who was on the Field* (Manchester: David Jones Society, 1979), p. 12.

8 Ibid, p. 20.

9 These stories, which I heard Jones relate sometimes more than once are recorded more or less as I heard them by William Blissett in *The Long Conversation, A Memoir of David Jones* (Oxford: Oxford U.P., 1981).

10 Martin Middlebrook, *The First Day on the Somme* (New York: Norton, 1972), pp. 68, 86.

11 *A History of the 38th (Welsh) Division*, p. 15. Jones indicates in the margin of his copy that he was involved in this raid 'as part of the covering troops. To be part of a raiding-party you had not only to volunteer but be judged the kind of person best suited for the job. I was not considered suitable'.

12 The men of Jones's battalion had not, at this time, participated in or witnessed an assault, and so may not have realized the extraordinary nature of their method of assault on this occasion.

13 Middlebrook, pp. 175, 137-8.

John Davies
The Visitors' Book

I.

Just where along the line did this voice start
chirping *cheerio* and *chap*, my language
hopping the frontier? Things fall apart,

the sentry cannot hold. Distant, he will keep
barking 'Where d' you think you are, boy? On stage?
Back of the gwt!' My cover, see, isn't deep:

my *ear/year/here* you couldn't tell apart.
Should I say 'I'll do it *now*', don't bank on it.
And still some words seem unusably upstart:

brouhaha sounds like the Tory Hunt tearing fox
-gloves. *Rugger* too. I can't say *Dammit*
or ride phrases trotting on strong fetlocks.

These days, language slouching through me lame
from the States is – well, a whole new ballgame.

2.

Cymmer Afan: wet pensioned streets fagged-out
claim only drifting is possible here.
At journey's end, no surge but smoke, no sound
from the deep except some lorry's threshing.

I was towed dreaming on this stretch, years back,
a boxed childhood bobbing between high walls,
then steel's fist pulled the plug on coal
so I was flushed down to Port Talbot.

No, on the whole I don't think I'd go back –
though I do for the usual half-reasons
and took my daughter once. Like me, perhaps
she'd pick up the sonar blips. Nettle-stung,
she proved only the seer's point that one's
Lost Valley is just another's vale of tears.

3.

There was Ossie Beynon. He was no good.
He had a kick like a pussy cat, hands
allergic to leather. He ran when he could.

There was Ron Beynon, tightly in cahoots
with fear. A twitch inching at full-back,
tethered there, he was known as Pissin Boots.

Fred Beynon too. The prop. What can I say?
I have seen him, fag-flushed, urge on his pack
from a safe mudpatch twenty yards away.

And their dad, I remember, the weaver
of teams. Ranting, he never missed a match,
all pally valour in his valley pallor.
He watched them glide on fields of praise
and loved their sharp finesse, their gutsy ways.

4.

Now big bad Hywel, Giant of Afan,
challenged the far-off giant Mog to fight
then slunk bedwards as his jitters began.

His boots like sheds he'd left outside the house.
Mog knocked. Said Hywel's wife: 'Ssh, why frighten
the child?' – showing those boots. And Mog turned mouse.

Since then I've known a lot of folk (mostly
non-giants) hang out large gestures at the door
and thrilled at their mastery of touch-and-go.
Trouble is, Mog came back later quietly…

Still, even when your bold front *is* another's,
chancing your voice instead of giving all
to giant Silence seems best, making close calls
your guests – the art of poetry amongst others.

5.

'Why can't poems be clearer? This one
of yours –' Even now my mother can make me jump.
That afternoon, by car, we tracked sunlight
to hazed terraces where Cymmer tumbled
half in the flustered river, where the house
once ours blinked its bay window modestly.

While she went visiting, I could make out
the road's allusions to stone, obscure trees,

up where it pencilled lines about the heat
on grass. Still I'm unsure just how far
to follow it. We talked of the street
later, people we'd known way back. And briefly
they shimmered in the windscreen, stars
almost there as I took the sky's veiled slack.

6.

A sonnet's no shape for the geography
or life round here, you say: too cool, too neat
by half for these valleys' buzz and heat.
Hell, you've been reading again, Welsh Disney
stories full of Dai Oddball in a whirr
clean out of his mine, a hwyl-happy freak
down the Con Club proving plotless weeks
don't happen. I've had him up to here.

As for geography, this stretch of valley
narrowed my focus fast. See how the slopes rhyme
mirror-like to the Afan's tidy rhythm?
How everything runs down in symmetry?

No. Well... I've been away too long
to catch the place's rough and ready song.

Glyn Jones
Shader's Vision

Shader, unable to sleep, and browsing through his heap of books, has a vision of fair women, his own country's and other's, which recalls the sighs of his wasted youth.

Where is Tangwen now, where Nest, where is Gwenllian,
The apple-blossom and the summer's glow?
Where are the 'gentle, gold-torqued maidens of
This Island'? Where is Elen of the Hosts?
Sun-bright Elen under her diadem,
Gold and rubies and imperial stones?
Mantled Elen in her milk-white silk, clasped
And girdled with red gold – yellow-haired Elen
Of excelling beauty, on her golden throne,
Her cheek upon her sleeping Emperor's cheek?
Where is Lleucu now, where Gwen, where golden Angharad?
Where are Betty Blythe, and Vilma Banki, and Laura La Plante?
Where Eryl, the goddess – her stare,
Her hauteur, that we, her worshippers, believed could halt
Chemistry at the confines of her body?
Where Rhiannon, enchantress, whose beauty crashed about
                                        our flesh,
Blazing, golden as shattered nets of torn-down
Lightnings to catch us thunderstruck and staggered?
Slake me in moon-showers, cool Llio, crazy, I cried,
Wipe me in rainbows of your moon-mist loveliness.
Where is Olwen, where Branwen, where Brengain?
Where Morfydd – her honeyed hair, her unshawled shoulders,
Her marbled arms, beneath which nature,
With accustomed insensitivity,
Had placed a heavy tuft of low-grade hair?
Where is Pola Negri – Pola, the tingle of your teeth
Like cavalry, your lips like couches?
Where all the beautiful and high-class girls
Who let us finger them in the dark lanes of our village?
I have seen them since, tired in city supermarkets,

Thick nosed, afflicted, grey, called Nana, buying
Cut-price toilet rolls in large quantities.
And lovely Mabli of the mental hospitals,
Mabli, dying alone in smelling sun, in the glass
Corridors of her mind's reclusion,
Grey-bearded, her lids down, silently
Wetting herself – and my voice brings some
Tapping past upon her heart's abandoned panes,
And the anguished inmate, wild-eyed exile,
Rouses, croaking, 'Jesus Christ, the same
Yesterday, today, and for ever', – where
Is her lovely striding, her high laugh, her molten
Leopard-leap of wit and silken winds lifting
Her gold-red hair, sea-winds above her ears
Lifting that sunlight-polished gold, word-
Drowning breeze between us on the sunlit beach -
And I awake again to hear, 'Jesus Christ, the same
Yesterday, today, and for ever', – and
I feel the shit-soaked feathers beat about my face,
The screeches wake me and the talons tear my heart.

As Shader rises, weeping, to close and replace his
Mabinogion, his glance alights upon a *cywydd* couplet in a
book of poems fallen open from the untidy pile heaped on
his attic floor–

> *Pa beth ydyw byw a bod?*
> *Nwyd ofer, yna difod.*

Ruth Bidgood
Hawthorn at Digiff

When I was a child, hawthorn
was never brought into our house.
It was godless to throw a pinch
of spilled salt, or dodge ladders,
yet no-one ever carried in
the doomy sweetness of red may or white.

Down there by the river,
shivering with heat, is Digiff,
a house full of hawthorn. The tree
grows in the midst of it, glowing
with pale pink blossom, thrusting
through gaps that were windows,
reaching up where no roof
intervenes between hearth and sky.

On the hill, sun has hardened
old soggy fields below the bluebell woods.
Rusty wire sags from rotten posts.
Outcrops, couchant dinosaurs, share
rough comfort with a few unshorn sheep.
Below, gardens have left their mark.

I bring a thought into this day's light
of Esther and Gwen, paupers:
Rhys and Thomas, shepherds: John Jones,
miner of copper and lead:
who lived here and are not remembered,
whose valley is re-translated
by holiday bathers across the river,
lying sun-punched: by me:
by men who keep a scatter of sheep
on the old by-takes.

At Digiff is hawthorn on hearth and bed-place.
Seen close, the tree is flushed

with decay. Sick lichened branches
put out in desperate profusion
blossom that hardly knows
an hour of whiteness before slow dying
darkens it. This is that glowing tree
of doom and celebration,
whose cankered flowers I touch
gently, and go down to the ford.

Christine Evans
Out of the Dark

I am the last night of August, late.
Under the sycamores darkness is so full
it cannot sleep. Four fields away the sea
dreams of suffocation.
The barley's schoolgirl heads
are bowed and waiting.

I am globular and slow.
My pores ooze salt and honeydew.
There is red wine still
at the corners of my mouth.
I feel the white rose arching to the moment
her petals peel and fall.

Ripe flesh hangs heavy;
drags back to the earth.

Towards dawn, I turn into a fat pale moth
blundering through cowbreath air
pressing myself against windows
seeking cracks in bedroom doors
to let slip the petals of my wings
where winter will not scatter them
before they are read.

In sea and trees and barley
and in your twisted sheets
I sweat and sigh.

I am the pause
between filling and flowing
the hush
at the heart of bursting
I am all roundness
beginning to wrinkle
to blur at the edges with fever
to pucker and seep

and I ache to be sharpened
to be picked, to be eaten
sliced back to the core
by the breath of the Arctic

rubbed clean like a new moon
to be angular, lithe
to be thin as a flash
windblown and buried

to be quickened

To come out of the dark
breathing clear horizons, wider skies

To be September.

Tony Curtis

William Orpen & Yvonne Aubicq in the Rue Dannon

This morning he wakes early –
sun and the sound of carts in the streets
coming though the roughly-drawn curtains,
a fine March light over the city.
She has lain an arm across his shoulder.
In sleep her beauty is muted, held somewhere

ringing like the glint of a far-off bell.
He has seen them in ruins, the churches,
the chateaux, the empty, crumbling town squares.
He has coloured them green against brown,
yellow against dirt, the torn bodies,
the green limbs under shell-hole water.
He dreamt of lobsters moving behind glass
in the restaurant at the Savoy.
Yvonne stirs under his breath,
her sleeping face turns halfway to his.
The head is perfect under night-tousled hair,
her eyelids shimmer like butterflies' wings.
There is painting and life and death.
The mayor's beautiful daughter lies in his bed.
He is having a good war.

Last August baked the mud of the Somme
into a pure, dazzling white. And there
were daisies, blood-red poppies
and a blue flower, for miles it seemed,
great masses of blue that were,
close-to, particular delicacies.
The sky a pure, dark blue and the whole air
for thirty feet up or more quivered
with white butterflies.

I brushed them – I was gentle – from
my uniform as I returned to the car.
We drove on through fields of white crosses,
the butterflies slamming against my driver's glass,
as if those crosses lurched out of the unsettled earth.

At Thiepval I began to paint a trench.
It held the remnants of two soldiers
– one German, one of ours.
I could not hold the sight for too long at a time
so gave myself rest against the torn trunk of a tree.
Three sessions, an hour passed, and then
a loose shell came over and burst.

I was blown backwards head over arse.
My heavy portrait easel took the force
– a skull smashed up through the canvas –
and the whole scene was blown to hell.

He slips away from her embrace
and she murmurs in sleep.
Tomorrow or the next day it will be complete –
the light on that slope of her left shoulder,
more work on the hair perhaps. He'll
watch her comb it as he loads his palette.
He has caught her classically
holding herself back from one's gaze,
arms crossed over her breasts
pulling her robe to her right shoulder.
That teasing look will devastate.

He rises, wraps the robe about himself
and crosses to the window to light a cigarette.
From the balcony he blows smoke over Paris.

At the end of the Rue Dannon is a square.
This is where they will march her – yes
I'll say she is a spy – call her Frida Neiter –
a spy for the Boche that the French will shoot.
She does not scream or struggle,
but walks upright, across the road
to the wall.
As the soldiers raise their rifles and
the officer his sword, she lets
slip her fur coat to the ground.
Naked she stands to face them,
her arms held out from her sides.

It seems a lifetime before they fire.

Dannie Abse
Hotel Nights

In the Angel Hotel

In the Angel Hotel no images allowed,
no idols. Artists, leave before midnight!

Do not strike a match in the dark laboratories
of Sleep where tomorrows are programmed.

Do not dream of stone shapes or listen to stone's
unauthorised version of silence.

Names have destinies. Write your own. Do not forge
a known sculptor's in Sleep's Visiting Book.

Else boulders will crash down. Like wood, malice of stone:
wood once took revenge on a carpenter's son.

Ignore the celestial light from the street outside,
the thud and beating of wings in the corridor

Now read the instructions in the event of fire.
Note the nearest exit door. Sleep well.

In the Royal Hotel

Should you wake up from the usual underworld
at 3a.m. wondering where you are, why you are,

it is fitting that you recall those adventurers
who journeyed far to meet a favoured guru.

Sheba was one such. She crossed mountain ranges,
sky-filled rivers just to hear Solomon's wisdom.

She sojourned in tents without air-conditioning,
without those other extras this hotel provides:

colour TV, Radio 2, herb-foam bath crystals,
that essential fridge stacked with refreshments.

She arrived, at last, to record the first wise words,
changed into her jewelled apparel, unaware

that three glass walls surrounded his gloden throne.
And thinking shimmering reflections to be water

she raised her skirts daintily, regally approached.
Then the great king rose slowly, as if astounded.

Clutching his glittering crown with his left hand,
hesitated, then cried out, 'You have hairy legs!'

You who would seek out such sages and seers
for secret truths wrapped in obscurity, mark this.

In the Holiday Inn

After the party I returned to the hotel.
The room was too hot so I took off my coat.

It was January but I turned down the thermostat.
I took off my shirt but I was still too hot.

I opened the window, it was snowing outside.
Despite all this the air began to simmer.

The room had a pyrexia of unknown origin.
I took off my trousers, I took off my shorts.

This room was a cauldron, this room was tropical.
On the wall, the picture of willows changed

to palm trees. In the mirror I could see the desert.
I stood naked in my socks and juggled

with pomegranates. I offered offerings
that soon became burnt. This was some holiday.

I took off one sock and read the bible.
They were cremating idols, sacrificing oxen.

I could feel the heat of their fiery furnace.
I could hear those pyromaniacs chanting.

I could smell the singed wings of cherubim.
I took off the other sock and began to dance.

Like sand the carpet scalded my twinkling feet.
Steam was coming out of both my ears.

I was King David dancing before the Lord.
Outside it was snowing but inside it was Israel.

I danced six cubits this way, six cubits that.
Now at dawn I'm hotter than the spices of Sheba.

What shall I do? I shall ask my wise son,
Solomon. Where are you Solomon?

You are not yet born, you do not know
how wise you are or that I'm your father

and that I'm dancing and dancing.

Peter Finch
Bigheads

Bighead
Executive bighead
Senior bighead
Southern development bighead
Bigheads, publish with us
Bigheads needed, send sample

Competition, thousands of bigheads to be won
World famous bighead will analyse your work
Try us, bigheads, we're cheap
Abu Dhabi touring bighead
128K computer bighead
Sales bigheads
Neo-Georgian bigheads
Elegant commode bigheads
New natural colour bighead
Bargain bighead
Uncensored bigheads, send no cash
Continental bigheads in full bighead positions
Bigheads under plain cover
Swing along bighead
You, me and the bighead
Race ahead all-British bighead
Soft bighead
Quilted nylon bighead
Bighead accessories
Folding bighead
Turn your bighead into a bidet
Blocked bighead
Bighead with Queen Anne legs
Shy bighead
Quality leather bighead
Rotproof bighead
Magnified bighead
A bighead on a string

A sward is:

a) a weapon
b) an absorbent pad

or

c) a bighead

Traditional bigheaded wrought-iron arse pole
500 bigheads given away free
Taming Of The Bighead
The Bighead In Winter
Roget's Bighead
The Secret Bighead Of Adrian Mole
The Bighead's Yearbook
The Oxford Companion to Bigheads
Valley Of The Bigheads
The Guinness Book Of World Bigheads
Jonathan Livingstone Bighead
How Bigheaded Was My Valley
There Are No Bigheads In My Valley Now

Today is your birthday
Your stars indicate over-optimism and
bigheadedness
Before you rush into the bigheaded business of
playing
cat and bighead with another's affections, check if
they are not a bighead too.

Dunlop latex bigheads
Gigantic winter bigheads
Clean up your bigheads
Ban unmarried bigheads
Keep bigheads off tv

Spot the bighead among the following:

a) Gillian Bighead
b) Tony Bighead
c) Chris Bighead
d) John Cowper Bighead
e) Robert Bighead
f) Ifor Bighead
g) John Bighead Bighead
h) Bighead ap Bighead
i) Myfanwy ap Tudur Bighead

j) Kingsley Amis

Only bigheads may enter
Winners will not be notified
they will already know

Glyn Jones

Envoi

Old, I watched the darling swallow families gathering,
Their fringes perched, spaced out, along the village wires,
Each sweet bird black, no wider than an eyelash – why
Should these bring molten to my throat so old a heart?

Blessing, I saw their swift flight above radiant hayfields,
           it was warm
And summer then, in hundreds they wove their invisible
           silkiness above
The standing hay (their weft swift, it was the wennol of
           the waterside weavers),
Or they ruggered unstoppable down wings of the blinding
           meadows,
They were reckless, their headlong speed, as though defy-
           ing calamity, rocked them – "Be careful,
Dear things", I wished to cry out in warning at such
           consummate lunacy –
The wheezing machinery of their tiny cries the sweetest
           of birdsong;
Black and white in their beauty, in their rashness they
           licked out sleek wings,
They were dark, they were glossy, rigid the symmetry of
           their forked tail feathers.

Now it is all over. They gather on the high wires
           twittering in excitement
To be gone in this gloom. Goodbye, you were the lovely
           white lilac birds,

Your flocks flying into our wastelands trawled here warmth
From the longed-for south, from the lands where sunlight
                    falls
Bright on dark skins, brilliant on the beauty of the dappled
                    antelope,
On olives and honey, balm, oil and barley – early figs
Are there also and heavy gold leaking everywhere from sun-
            lit trees.
Goodbye, goodbye, you were about us in sunlight, swift,
Bright as the astonishment of youthful perceptions –
            lovely as glancing epiphanies
The gaiety of your visitations; and now you prepare joyfully
            to leave us,
Heedless you take off for ever, you are visions and images,
The words and their dazzle, you leave me bereft, darling
            birds,
You will fly elate under rainbows, forgetful of us beneath
            great girders of the grey clouds –
Where did you ponder the gospels of that strict navigation? –
Night travellers joyful beneath jewelled harness of darkness,
Hurling yourselves at hot suns risen smoking before you
Or burying brilliance in the panes of their waters, and you
Exultant between emptiness blue above and below you.

Mist and darkness begin now to gather and the small rain
            falls heavily –
And here with the sad, with the finished, fleeting enchanters,
            you leave me,
With the rain and the ruffian wind rising and these shabby
            old men standing bowed all about me –
Who are these grey mutterers? – ach, hateful, rancid,
With thick glasses and ear-plugs, grey hairs and holes in
            their trousers –
Oh, birds, darling thieves and bewitchers, at your going
            we are weary, sad,
We are sick and defeated, all are abandoned, with tears
            on our cheeks
And with great weights heavy on our heart.

John Ormond
Waiting in the Garden

If down into the green glaze
Of this evening garden suddenly cascaded
No less than angels, having been first
White hesitations, a small suggestion of cloud,
Then raggedly spiralling, trying to find formation,
Finally falling to be material, wingtip feathers
Transparent alabaster;

The beginners, good boys killed on their motorbikes,
In novices' nightshirts, shaming
The smiling patriarchs – who died before
The Bible was set down – as they clip
The tops of the lilac-trees, crash-landing a-clatter
In the rhubarb, snapping the stems off short,
Breaking their legs yet again.

What would I say if the aged, approaching,
Rubbing their shins, uttered "Come",
And then repeated it, "Come, come. We come to take you
To where the secret is"? Of course, I would ask
For their credentials; and they'd produce
From inside zipped-up pockets the required
Flying licences, innoculation forms and gilt IDs;

The old white-parsley-bearded flight-lieutenants
Delving for scuffed quill-written jobs
On parchment. They'd begin: We the Archangel Gabriel,
Foreign Secretary of Heaven, Request and Require...
And then their images, illuminated, faded Byzantine,
Their Wing-Commander, meanwhile, smiling a small smile,
Remembering how many abortive sorties he's flown.

And the young, the latest-risen from cooling blood,
Presenting their baffled grins from postage stamps

Of pictures taken in booths in the far corners
Of celestial Woolworths. You can see them jostling,
Fussing their hair, finessing with gold combs,
Crowding for next turn, excited. Smile, flash,
Smile, flash, 2, 3, 4. The curtain then drawn back,

And then the waiting.
What answer do they bring?
What answer not yet given by the evening light
And the questions and pleasantnesses
At the table in the green of this lady's garden?
And the strong white house, its books and pictures,
The questions and children I have pondered in it?

Would my most welcome visitors, awkwardly ascending
From their failed mission, be stripped
Of their silver stripes, be Heaven-bound not grounded,
Confined to base, forfeit their harps? I'd hope not.
Poor lucky souls, knowing the mystery.
I'd signal them "Good luck,
Good flying" as the garden darkened.

Catherine Fisher
Noah

Forty Days

This is the almost legendary hour.
Outside, the world dissolving;
around me the seeds of animals
sleep the cold sleep.

The fractious woman slumbers;
my restless boys, tight
in their dreams. Only
the old man listens.

I am frail flotsam; timbers
swollen on the tide.
It has been forty centuries
since I stood upright.

My craft is pitted, aimless,
arrival now not to be thought of;
stillness, no motion,
strange solidity underfoot.

I would be wary of such cessation;
if the movement should stop.
It was in silence
the voice spoke before.

Hearing it now would be wreckage,
splintered on a reef of sunlight,
the doors stove in by rainbows,
livestock cascading after my raven and dove.

Firmament

Slowly spinning, the probe descends.
This is the second he has sent;
Raven is lost.

He has no radio contact; in
the vacuum of stars and dust,
cannot afford failure.

The blurred orb beneath him is now
                              untouched.
He carries the seed that will sow it,
garner its alien harvest.

Despite this, he is old,
cannot forget the faces in the lost towns.
Because of that we chose him.

No world is new. Even this, rising
from its receding waters, is only the old,
washed, ready to try again.

Deluge

Today it rains roses and African violets,
purple spinning petals
piled upon the wheelhouse and the deck
and this round window.
Forty days of gulls and meteorites,
and water.

Tonight it rains acid on trees in Norway,
etching the windows of log-houses
with strange hieroglyphs,
unreadable for generations.
Forty days of runes and crystals,
and dead leaves.

In deserts it rains dust and locust,
the dry dessicated itches
of skin and throat
flaking on the sun's anvil.
Forty days of thirst and blowflies,
and stones for bread.

Here it rains cats and dogs, frogs,
old woman with sticks.
No portent would be missing
in the world's delirium.
Forty days of falling angels,
and a white dove.

Adrift

Drive them up to Pen-y-Bwlch
he said, the slow herd

with their chiming guide,
woolly with indirection.

When did the snow begin?
The glaze on my face is hours old;
these five sticks in the woollen glove
no longer mine.

Constriction round the heart,
ice in the beard; my mouth two
wooden slats warped and illfitting,
hammered askew.

I wear the white coat, the cold wool.
It lies unshearable on earth's shoulders;
my flock mites in the fleece, drowned
in the stiffened surge.

Body moulds this blue-white chamber,
bedded with animals, aching
bell silent. When did I last thrust the
dove of my hand to the air?

Drowsy, we wait the spade
shattering our crystal, the gasping
stars, the white astonished
world at our feet.

Ararat

I, Otto, write the last entry.
The forward shaft is flooded,
holed on rock. The sea

engulfs us. Schmidt is dead,
and the others, lost in the ruined city.
Perhaps I will see them yet.

I have just been down to the crew deck; they
sit silent as beasts. Paulson said
they trust me. Me.

The order came, it had to be followed.
God knows, no-one wanted this journey,
me included.

I think of Anna's letter.
"After the turmoil, the calm sea.
Believe the future will be better."

And now the future is here;
we must rise to meet it. We must open
the hatches. And we must surrender.

Tony Conran
Giants

A castle is a wedge in the soul.

He had purchase from it,
Leverage
Like a pair of forks back to back
To divide
The warm belonging root of us.

I climb now to the Earl's opposite.

★★★

Up the sharp scree, up the lace alb
Of the hill, stepping
Where disks of rhyolite chink,
Up to the bleached skeleton
Of a hill-fort, laid out
On a limb of Yr Eifl
Under the running cloud.
Tre'r Ceiri we call it, town of giants.

Really, the giants are us,
Denizens larger than life
Of the erected scree. While we live
Each of these cauldrons of dry stone
Is capped like a kraal. Smoke
Twists its way through birch bark.
Moans of oxen hang round us like mist.

While we live, these parapets stand.

Cashel or rath, hillforts of
Dry stone or earth ramparts,
Clan homes, gathering places,
Shrines of the gods. Are our hearts
Littered here, is this where
The bones gasp and tear themselves in
                              parturition
Among the starry tormentil
When we are brought forth – giants
And whole men, women whole as day?

Duncan Bush
Two Poems of Victor Bal

The Leader

Fabulous beast, father, in our dreams we
wonder sometimes if you really do
exist. One gives you six legs
like an insect, or a thousand like

a battalion. Another, a dragonfly's
wings, and an ant-coloured
Assyrian beard; and in your plaited
beehive hat, a multitude of

layered cells, more rooms than
the Palace of Soviets or the Hotel Moskva,
each one a perfect hexagon.
That swarming is

your thoughts. But, like everyone, I
must think I dream you as
you truly are: seeing you always
on a medal round your own neck, but

ubiquitous as coin: half-profiled
bas-relief of bronze stone gazing right,
shrewd-eyed into the future, the future
some of us won't see.

Bal's poem 'The Leader' makes reference to two buildings, the Palace of Soviets and the Moskva Hotel. Since the poem was written (probably in 1935) the architectural history of Moscow has served only to increase any dimension of irony in these allusions to the building programme of the Stalin years.

The Palace of Soviets was intended to be the ultimate statement of megalomania in public building. The largest architectural structure in the world, it was to be built in honour of Stalin's first Five Year Plan, and to accommodate Party Congresses, meetings of the Supreme Soviet, etc. Besides a vast number of offices, it would also contain restaurants and other amenities, and two huge halls with seating for 20,000 and 8,000 respectively. Situated within view of the Kremlin, on the site of the demolished Cathedral of the Redeemer, its ground area was 10,000 square metres. The cement used in the foundations amounted to sixteen percent of the annual output of the Soviet Union. The projected central section was to be a quintuple-tiered skyscraper tower surmounted by a massive statue representing the liberated proletariat. This was later replaced by a plan for a statue of Lenin, the dimensions of which were to be enlarged from the original eighteen metres to seventy-five metres in height, the entire palace acting as a pedestal for this gigantic statue. After several years of revision to the plans, it was intended that building would start on January 1, 1935, but it was not until 1937 that final changes were accepted. Early in the construction work a major difficulty with water seepage arose, as might have been expected in a low site so close to the river. The base was covered with bitumen in a futile attempt to counteract this problem. Nevertheless, by 1941 the huge steel skeleton of the building began to rise above the city. Now, however, it was the wartime emergency coupled with the increasingly insoluble problem of the insecure foundation, which suspended the work, though the plans for the building were never officially abandoned. As war continued, the shortage of steel led to the skeleton being gradually dismantled, piece by piece for use in the war effort. In 1960 a swimming pool was constructed over the foundations of the intended palace.

The Moskva Hotel is an impressive if somewhat monumental edifice of granite and concrete on Moscow's Okhotny Ryad. Designed by the architects

A.V. Shchusev, L.I. Savelyev and O.A. Stapran, it was completed in 1935. Despite its imposing portico and piers, which dwarf passers-by in the street below, the facade of the building has come to represent a grim joke in that the left and right wings of its frontage – each one twelve storeys in height – are completely different in design and look mismatched. Apparently Stalin was shown a plan in which the front elevation offered two variants in juxtaposition. Failing to notice this, Stalin approved the plan as it stood. No one dared point out the error, and the building was completed to incorporate both designs.

Night, Day

We lie awake at night and dream
the knocking at the door through which
we'll disappear for ever. By day, commune
our fate and share deliverance with

surprising crowds left on the pavements still.
By the Kremlin wall, too, a queue lengthens
in patience, as if to view
the reliquary calf's blood and pig's bones

of Christ. While with every swivel-perfect
change of guard, even Lenin,
waxen in the mausoleum, thinks
that they have come for him at last.

Landeg White
Immortal Diamond

(Jack Mapanje, detained 25 September, 1987)

Outside the bar, night, bullfrogs promising rain,
the sky a dome of stars ripped
by the black edge of the mountain.

Bloated face, trunk like a baobab,
"We've got your lame friend"
from the unmarked jeep

boasting Special Branch. Words hidden
a hemisphere off grudge
"Now you're on your own,"

and I can smell, here, the Carlsberg
on his breath. He leers
from the smuggled page.

Lame: alone: "We're
preparing a place for him."
This clown knows the power

of pauses, the ecstasy of rhythm.
His threat is accurately
their dread. For Jack, our dear friend's poems

are out, unparolled, his meta-
phors dancing from lip
to lip and no heavyweight

knuckles ripping
pages
can stop

them. The crippled swagger,
"We've got your friend,"
calms outrage

at that night, that frog-loud prison yard, leaned
on by the mountain, where Jack, joke, patch
matchwood, hardens

like starlight, needing no crutch.

Steve Griffiths
Elegy for John Tripp

A man on the radio talked of soft tissue
printed on a millon-year riverbed
like a morning-after mattress –

and I thought of you very clear, John,
lifting a pint of dark in some dolmen basement
regarding the sudden answers of the morning
after stealing away, your sharp face
set in that spirit of mock astonishment
you learned to bewilder
producers of talks and tired assumptions.

I remembering a belated urgency
in your face, as it turned back
watching the cultivation of soft edges,
as history, its fares paid, took off like a taxi
we tried to hail with a borrowed carafe.
There was a march full of friends' banners
and irony, probably sodden,
with a brass band and cock-up somewhere.

On a stand in another world
the unprofitable take an unremitting review
of their leaders.
You take the salute, spilling drinks
and blood and atonement, and you break the silence
with what nearly everyone felt,
snarling at flummery, throned, waxing manic
then tender as warm buns in a paper bag
with some small forgiven fault
from your recognised gallery.

Confusion and moral astonishment,
something unfinished, an obvious instruction
unlearned: you listened and stirred tea
to the huge roaring ironies
of shopping-bag conversation
as the rust-red deep shit rose at the window.

Then you slotted the poems accurately
in the darkness between laughing teeth
in darkened smokefilled rooms

like some young boy who, they said, had
'immaculate positional play';
like the occassional sun through the steamy
windows of your café,
illuminating the brown sauce and the salt.

And you planted your ground of demands
that you never sold
for one moment of narrow-angled comfort,
brambles round tanks.
Your green armies
knitted their sharp-eyed peace,
needling hard minds,
weaving, digging, planting,
still they work and plot:
they move down out of the hills' cover
laughing their experienced laugh.

Duncan Bush
Bardot in Grangetown

Off Ferry Road, the toilet garage where
the mechanics come at lunch to cut the hands' grease
with green jelly, glancing once

at themselves in the rust-foxed mirror, and then
go in to eat brought sandwiches and play
pontoon with the soft, soiled pack,

three walls of the cubicle sporting the odd grey
newsprint pinup, some Kay or Mandy,
alike as playing cards,

and then a whole closed door facing you if
ever you sat over the stained bowl
of Bardot as she was at twenty,

and thirty-five, and is now, still corn-blonde,
and then more of her

again (with one of Ian Rush) out where they eat,
over the workbench's oil and
hacksaw-dust, the clenched vice.

The boy who put all hers up was a six-month Government
trainee. A bit simple, they all thought.
A headbanger, the fat one said.

He had a thing about her, the boy, grinning
foolishly, half-proudly, if they kidded him or told him
she was old enough to be

his mother. *That slag?* the fat one said once.
*Look at her. She's anybody's. Even saving baby seals
all she knows how to do*

is lie down with one. And laughted: soft, smirched face
looking at that photograph, then at one of
her naked, hands raised as if to pin or

loose her hair, the honey-hued, still-teenage
body, milky Mediterranean behind her, evening.
He left the other week,

the trainee. He didn't finish, he never even came
back for his tools. So now they're
anybody's, like the photos:

Like, the fat one knows, the photos always are.

John Barnie
I Had Climbed the Long Slope

I had climbed the long slope of the spur from Capel Madog to
                              Banc-y-Darren
Where hedgerows of whitethorn leaning away from the western
                                        wind

Thin out to be replaced by stiff fence-posts of weathered wood
That are always grey, strung with rusted barbed wire, for the last
                                                few miles.
On the field banks with their thin feathers of upland grass, hare
                                bells raised soft blue flowers
And bushes of gorse the rough intense green of their canopies.
Nobody walked here, and a wheatear ahead of me had a
                                        moorland tameness,
Flitting along fence-posts as I came, with its rich buff-and-grey,
                        black mask, black wings and tail.
On either side parallel ridges were grouped in rough lines and to
                                        the north
Cader Idris was a grey wash rugged with bulk.
In the summer light the sea's geometric plane canted up to the
                                        horizon where
So indistinct the eyes strained to believe them, the hills of Pen
                                        Llŷn
Were islands, a rubbing of deeper blues between sky and water.
On the highest point of the ridge I'd stopped to look back, then
                                        turned
To the six houses of Banc-y-Darren strung at the throat
Of my ridge and the next, where I'd make my descent.
Out of the hills beyond, a speck hurtled ahead of itself,
A Phantom, nose tearing through the silk and pressure of the air.
In such a still world the eye follows anything that moves.
On across the valley parallel to where I stood,
It was beautiful as a harebell or a wheatear.
As it reached me, it was still ahead of its sound, as if its power
                                        were silence
Fuelled by the land its shadow fled across.
I could see the tanks slung under the wings
And the two grey missiles
Slim and leaning at the end of the tightened leash.
And through the clear canopy I saw Cader Idris beyond
And that the Phantom was empty.
Then the power of the engine buckled and crumpled the air,
Sound chasing this marvel which sped ahead in perfection.
It diminished to a spot until I knew it must be over the sea,

And when my sight felt that almost it must snap
And that now I could see it and now not, the Phantom fell in the
                                        slowest of curves,
Its fuel tanks exhausted.
The earth around me had absorbed the shock of the engine
And now in the sea there was a short white punctuation
That rose to a silent spume, then settled back
In the canted water.
The wheatear still flicked ahead of me from fence to fence
And I walked on to Banc-y-Darren
Past the few mountain ash that every year
Try out leaves above branches and trunks
That will never be more than crippled in the poor soil of these
                                        fields.
And I passed, on either side of the lane,
Houses with names and ordinariness,
Flowerbeds and cars, the modernized cottage and the
                                picture-window bungalow,
Everything as it ought to be, yet right and not right,
As if, though there would be deaths, there would also be days
People living here would call "tomorrow", with confidence.

Gwyneth Lewis

Going Primitive

Who can resist a didgeridoo
in the middle of Queen St. – not one, but three
from the Northern Territory,
each one more deeply, eucalyptically rude?

For the builders have lost their passers-by
who are drawn like water to the swirl and squelch,
the monstrous plumbing of his breath,
sucked in and further, and then atomised,

breathed out in stiff shirts and office skirts
but feeling looser...
A wasp photographer
snaps the man at all angles for something sweet

and the women, who sweat at his embouchure,
grow broad as rivers to his narrow lips,
dirty as deltas, with silting hips
and alluvial bosoms. The men, unsure,

cower behind their totem wives,
puny and trouty; now chimpanzees
swing through the scaffolding with ease
and screech with the newly arrived macaws;

cranes buck and bow and the wooden thrum
makes men recall a biography
of sludge and savannah, how it was when the sky
arched its blue back and started to come.

Edwin Morgan
Hands On, 1937

John S. Clarke, festooned with snakes, said, "Touch one,
look closely, they're quite beautiful; not slimy;
come on, come down to the front now, that's better.
Don't be afraid, girls, aren't these eyes pure jewels?
Come on lads, stretch your hands out, try this johnny,
I bet it's like no creature you ever handled."
I thought the lecture had been good, but this was
unforeseen, an unknown world, strange bonus –
the dry brown coil was at first almost leaden,
slightly rough but inert, with scales tight-fitting
like Inca walls, till what seemed a faint tickling
became a very crawling of the flesh as
movement began to test my arm, the ripples
of an almost unfathomable power

rhythmically saying, I am living:
you may not love me but oh how I am living!
And it is all one life, in tanks, bags, boxes,
lecture-theatres, outhouses, fronds of bracken,
rivers for men and serpents to swim over
from dark bank to dark bank and vanish quickly
about their business in raw grass and reedland,
scale, sole, palm, tail, brow, roving, brushing, touching.

Tram-Ride, 1939
F.M.

How cold it is to stand on the street corner
at nineteen, in the foggy Glasgow winter,
with pinched white face and hands in pockets, straining
to catch that single stocky gallus figure
who might be anyone but was one only;
prowling a few feet – not too far! – glanced at
idly by the patient Cosmo queue, growing
exposed, your watch burning, how long now, yes but,
what, half an hour, some eyes saying, Stood up, eh? –
until the step has to be taken, casually,
you have to stroll off, what's won by staying?
he won't appear (he had simply forgotten,
you didn't know that then), and on the top deck
of a southbound tram you stare into the window
as it reflects a mask about to shake with
ridiculous but uncontrollable tears, a choking
you gulp back instantly, no one has heard it,
shameful – shameful – to be dominated
by such emotions as the busy tramful
of half indifferent, half curious folk would
mock at if they knew, and would they sometime,
in half a century perhaps, accept that love is
what it is, that tears are what they are, that
Jack can shiver in the numbing close-mouth
of missing dates for Jill or Jake, and suffer?

A Feast

– But what am I to do with all these pumpkins?
– Bowl them to Hollywood to feed the turkeys!
– You know they fell from off the back of a –?
– No defence is needed. Sock it to them!
– Zombie pie and mumbling stew of cowboys?
– Have a slice of choking psychomania!
– Chew the creepy seeds of bloodless mutants?
– Bake a child of outer space for supper!
– A brunch of sleaze, well buttered in its batter?
– And one enormous car-chase tart for afters!
– But have we got the stomach for such crumbles?
– They've colourized the black and white, it's magic!
– Can you just wait to wolf that yellow ribbon?
– All those dark brown low-slung twitchy holsters!
– That brush-off in the heaving flesh-tint swimsuit?
– And one last slurp of siren-haunted sidewalk!
– Pyramids of punkins! Shall we bang them westward?
– Cram the turkeys. It's business and it's movies!

Lamps

And if anyone should tell our adventures,
remember that the universe has spaces
as well as forms – abysses, deserts, niches,
distances without even time as pedlar
to bring you, if you waited, explanations.
No, we have seen what we have seen, but often
there is a blank you must not fill with monsters.
It is all for what is to come after.
It is for the duguth of firm intent, the voyage
he and she and they must take, and you quiet
but trembling in your chair, rising, following
the light you catch, swinging but never vanishing,
into great deeps, our helmet-lamps, beckoning.

Michael J. Collins
The Gift of John Ormond

I FIRST MET JOHN ORMOND in October, 1974, when, on leave from the BBC, he and Glenys came to New York. Joe Clancy, then my neighbour on City Island, had asked me if I would arrange a reading at Fordham University, where I was working at the time, for someone named John Ormond, a visiting poet from Wales. I agreed to bring John to Fordham at the end of the month.

Although I have never admitted it to Joe, I was skeptical: I half-expected to meet that all too familiar figure on the academic landscape, someone calling himself a poet without ever having written anything that one would call a poem. I decided to find out just what sort of poet this John Ormond was. With her usual generosity, my mother, who was working in New York at the time, picked up on her lunch hour a copy of *Requiem and Celebration* at the Gotham Book Mart. (The newer collection, *Definition of a Waterfall*, was not on the shelves). As I read the poems in the second and third sections, I was amazed at what I found. Here was the real thing, a genuine poet with a mature and generous vision of the world and a language at once distinct, elegant, witty, and precise. I had not often read such individual, carefully crafted poetry. Within twenty minutes, I was impatient for his reading to begin.

And then I met the man himself, as engaging and distinct as the poems he wrote, energetic, passionate, laughing, full of life. During the reading which, he told us, was meant to be "an evening of serious cabaret," his resonant voice, his precise, idiosyncratic articulation turned the remarkable language of his poems in ways I had not expected. By the end of the evening, I had begun to know better both the poet from Wales and the superb poems he had read, and I never let either of them go again.

For the rest of John's life, as best we could with an ocean ordinarily between us, we remained friends. In his last years, when my work for Georgetown brought me to Europe, I was able from time to time to spend a day with John and Glenys in Cardiff and once, in May, 1987, a few consecutive days with John at Georgetown's villa in Fiesole, among Tuscan cypresses and olive trees, in that part of the world he loved so much. I wrote several essays on his poetry, largely in an effort to bring it the wider audience I believe it deserves. I enjoyed finding in print or receiving with a note from John the carefully crafted poems he released from time to time over the next sixteen years. I valued them for their deft and deceptively simple language and for their sustained attention, in a variety of tones and forms, to the fundamental religious question that seems to me to draw John's discreet poems into a distinctive and significant body of work. I read and re-read his poems with my students not only because they suggest what the craft of poetry entails, but because they seem to me to articulate, with powerful and profound regret, a compelling vision of the finite conditions by which we live, and yet to find, without ever denying those conditions, a ground upon which to celebrate the joy and beauty our lives inevitably bring us.

I continue to teach John's poetry in my classes at Georgetown not only because my students are moved by their generosity and beauty, but because it offers them "strong… words… against chaos," (Roland Mathias, 'Brechfa Chapel'), a "strong wall against winter," ('In September'), a vision that resists both equally debilitating certainties – presumption and despair. The poetry is valuable and worth the attention of the young men and women I teach because it looks unflinchingly at both the fragility of creation and the uncertainty with which we must inevitably live and, at the same time, remains generous, hopeful, grateful for all that is given, celebrating a world of time and change, lives that are given and taken away.

I have for many years now looked closely at 'Cathedral Builders' with first year pupils to help them see how its carefully structured progress brings order out of chaos, leads, in the words of Robert Frost, to "a momentary stay against confusion"; how the movement of the poem through time, from line to line and stanza to stanza, makes it an image, an analogy of the very things it describes; how its final line, "I bloody did that," is both the cathedral builder's and the poet's celebration of their craft, their looking up and back to what they have made and, like the creating God in Genesis, finding their work good.

I have read 'Cathedral Builders' at countless graduation ceremonies as well, hoping, with John's exquisitely modulated poem, not only to make a dean's required commencement address engaging and memorable, but to remind the graduates that whatever work we might do is both good and rewarding in itself and yet able, if we let it, to serve something beyond itself. In 'Cathedral Builders,' John articulates the vision that I suspect motivated and gave meaning to all his work, both as a film maker and a poet, a vision I hope might do the same for Georgetown's graduates as well – that our work, however satisfying, can be more than an end in itself, that it should be done, as Dylan Thomas put it, "for love of man and in praise of God." While I am not sure John could have himself said those last two words about his own work, 'Cathedral Builders' brings him close to the vision of Ignatius of Loyola, the founder of the Society of Jesus, a vision that inspired the work of the Jesuit poet Gerard Manley Hopkins and that inspires as well the work of Georgetown, a University founded by Jesuits.

As I read it to the graduates of Georgetown, the poem seems to me always a compelling articulation of the vision that has animated their course of study. 'Cathedral Builders' celebrates craftsmanship, making, labour, finds value and meaning in it, because it shares in and joins with God's work of creation and makes visible to a fallen world the beauty of what God has created and God's love for all that is. John might well be uneasy with so religious a reading of his poem, but not because he found himself, as he put it, unable to believe. (His own vision, like that of his poetry, seemed more complex and paradoxical than his simple statement suggests.) But even on its own terms, a religious reading of 'Cathedral Builders' claims too much, for it takes literally, as religious readings necessarily do, what may (or may not) be only metaphoric and so makes certain what the poem itself leaves uncertain. 'Cathedral Builders,' like so many of John's poems, finally rests delicately between yes and no, between life and loss, between eternity and time: making no absolute claims for transcendence, leaving such questions open, it celebrates the beauty and value of our works and days while recognizing the failings and fragility of all that is.

I have been teaching Shakespeare at Georgetown for many years now, both to twenty-year old undergraduates and to older men and women with a wide range of backgrounds and experience, and whenever I do, I look to John's wise and generous poems to help illuminate the plays. While the final scenes of Shakespeare's comedies, *As You Like It*, *Twelfth Night*, *Much Ado About Nothing*, even *Measure for Measure* and *The Tempest*, characteristically bring all their young lovers to putatively happy endings, they also simultaneously exclude others from that happiness and make felt, in various ways, the constraints of the finite world. Those odd and ambiguous endings inevitably recall one of John's early poems, 'Three Rs,' which he included in only one collection, *Requiem and Celebration*.

The last two lines of the poem, which is addressed to an unnamed "lover," to a man in love with and perhaps about to make love to a woman, hold in delicate balance the joy of love and the inevitability of loss: "Your brief and charmed arithmetic / Prove, for a time, that one and one is one." The gentle, parenthetical qualification, "for a time," breaking the rhythm of the lines, like Malvolio the steward moving off the stage at the end of *Twelfth Night*, vowing to be revenged, chastens the poem's triumphant celebration of human love with its whisper of time and change. The moving close of 'Three Rs' keeps the poem from presumption or despair, from claiming either too much or too little for a lovely yet fallen world. As Shakespeare recognized in his comedies, as John does in the little poem he wrote one night after work in the Amalfi, a restaurant in London, we who live in the mortal world find joy, but it remains subject always to our mortality.

If "golden time convents" (*Twelfth Night* 5.1.371), in the

real world as in the comedies, but for a moment, if every Romeo (and Juliet) must heed the song of the lark and leave the other for whatever Mantua claims them, what happiness might be possible for the young men and women I teach. John's poem, 'In September,' written, he said, in a night, when he had forgotten to buy an anniversary card for Glenys, sets out, in unassuming language and deceptively simple images, all that, if they are lucky, is possible for them. Romeo and Juliet need somewhere to rest after the ecstasy of their wedding night, and it ought not be Capulet's tomb or divorce court. The lovers who are joined at the end of Shakespeare's comedies (like the lovers who read them in my classes) need some vision of the future. The words of the speaker, John's words to Glenys, are words for every Romeo and Juliet to speak to one another twenty years after their balcony scenes, twenty years after their own romantic comedies have come to closure. I have discussed 'In September' again and again in my classrooms, I have read it at weddings, I have sent copies of it to students who have announced their engagements so that these young men and women might know what joy is possible in a fallen world, so they might neither ask too much of another fragile human being nor offer too little themselves.

The vision of the human condition in John's poetry, its precarious balance, the clear-eyed refusal to claim too much or too little for the mortal world and for the lives we live in it, are what I have come to value more and more in his poems. In teaching *King Lear*, when the Duke of Gloucester suddenly, unexpectedly, chooses to relieve the King and is blinded by Goneril and Regan for his compassion, I turn to a poem John once read to me at his dining room table, Glyn Jones's 'The Common Path,' for it seems to me to suggest what Shakespeare sees in Gloucester's choice, that we shall not save the world with the large, public gestures the nightly news reports, but by caring individually for the individuals we meet on the common path we walk each day.

But at the end of the play, as Lear kneels over the body of the dead Cordelia, asking us all, in the audience as well as on the stage, to "look there, look there" (5.3.312), I read some of John's own poetry with my students. What does Lear see? What does he ask us to look at? Some say he sees Cordelia living or at least sees something that tells him, despite her death, the world makes sense, justice will, in some mysterious way, get done. Others say he sees only what there is to see, the obscene insult of Cordelia's lifeless body. But the play says nothing, for it has chosen to be governed by the same conditions as govern the world it reflects, to bring its audiences to the very uncertainty with which, once they have left the theatre and returned to the world of their daily lives, they will inevitably live.

Some of John's most ambitious poems raise, in their own way, the fundamental religious question that *King Lear* raises: do we live finally in a sane or a lunatic universe? And the poems leave us where *King Lear* and our own lives leave us, with no word to answer the question, with the sense, to say it as John did, of a "lost word," the word that would allow, could we speak it, "the heart's short story" a certain telling. Poised between everything and nothing, between what is given and its inevitable loss, claiming neither too much nor too little for the world and the lives we live in it, John's poems finally, like the speaker in 'A Lost Word,' put by their "lust for secrets": "it is enough that the blade / Is sharp, that the sun lurks then rises over my garden's / Blown roses and its brown turmoil of leaves." All we shall ever know about ourselves and the world we shall discover in the existential turmoil of our lives, in our days of joy and sorrow. The only answers we shall have, as John puts it in 'Waiting in the Garden,' are those that can be "given by the evening light / And the questions and pleasantnesses / At the table in the green of this lady's garden."

While John's poetry never looks as closely as *King Lear* does at the horrors of the mortal world, I ask my students to ponder it in the context of that great play because, in its own way, it speaks with honesty and eloquence of the human condition, recognizing, as *King Lear* does, that we live without certainty, between life and loss, beauty and decay, joy and sorrow, eternity and time, meaning and chaos. In denying neither the conditions of our mortality nor the loveliness of the mortal world, neither our "lust for secrets" nor our inability to learn them, the poetry of John Ormond sees clearly the elemental uncertainty in which we live and thus provides a vision by which we might resist, in our own lives, both the blinding brilliance of presumption and the blinding darkness of despair. As John put it in a poem I have sent, far too often, to those who have lost, as we all do, one they have loved: "Enough that it was given, green, as of right, when, / Equally possible, nothing might ever have been."

When I realize, as I often do, that I shall not see John again, I listen to those lines from 'The Gift' and chasten my regret, as best I can, by remembering I have been greatly gifted and life made richer for knowing him. Although his poetry spoke repeatedly of the fragility of what we love, of the inevitability of time and change, I never quite connected the words he wrote with John himself: I always took for granted we would meet once again, in Cardiff, in Fiesole, or even in Georgetown.

As I think back over the sixteen years I knew him, I am surprised at how little time we actually spent together, how much our friendship depended on sporadic letters and, more recently, telephone calls. I regret John's health preventing his returning, as we both hoped he would, to Georgetown's villa in Fiesole so that he might have shared once again his poetry, his laughter, and his marvellous stories with our alumni there. I regret too that it never seemed possible to bring him to Georgetown to receive the honorary degree I intended to have conferred upon him and, as with anyone we love, that I did not have one last time to hear his voice before he died.

But, as John's poetry always affirms, life brings moments of joy as well as regret, and I shall remember always the great joy I felt when I visted John and Glenys in Cardiff on a warm and sunny Sunday in August, 1989. While I could not know it then, it would be the last time I saw John. After dinner, we were joined in the front room at 15 Conway Road by John and Glenys's daughter Rhian and Glyn and Doreen Jones. There, among family and friends, I had the honour to present John with a medal from Georgetown, on the occasion of its two hundreth anniversary, to thank him for his generous friendship to the University and to recognize his distingushed achievements as a poet and film maker. As I recall the end of that visit, my rushing out to catch the train back to London without, as is always the case, ever really getting the right words said, I am happy to think that I might have been able, with the medal and the formal words of citation, to tell John how much I owed him and how greatly I valued the poetry he wrote.

Shortly after we met, I published a short introduction to John's poetry in *World Literature Today*. At its end, I adapted some words of Yevgeny Yevtushenko to Robert Frost to suggest the profound impact the poetry had made upon me. Now, some sixteen years after I first read it, sixteen years after I first met him, those words still seem to me appropriate ones to say to John Ormond, an extraordinary poet and friend I shall remember always: "I have read your poems again and again today, I am glad you have lived on earth."

Christopher Meredith

Orang-utan

A radio sings. Too loud.
The children shout. Us.

In the old man's play no radio sings,
no children shout. After long stillness
he shuffles in his ragged gown upstage.
And the graceful falling, decorous heap,
each knotty, henna-ed rag disposed with art
fanned and folded as on a draped urn.
Behind the folds head vanishes floorward.
Right hand extends across the strawy stage.
The left goes upward. He doesn't look
but from old knowing fingers lock

the intersection of a crucifix
among the bars.
And still.
The tableau assembled.
He is perfectly composed. The ropes sway.
Leaves on his dying branches flicker once
and sunlight hardening after cloud
casts a lattice over him.
Technique's precise, disciplined as *noh*,
true and unreal
classical acting at its most exact.
Huge emptiness will not be broken
by the stirring of a hair or rib.

While elsewhere his usurping brother's
busy with a chainsaw, he, undaughtered,
without crown or book or staff or all the
places where he himself, holds the stage.
In the old man's play no radio sings.
No children shout. We are the fourth wall.

Glyn Jones
Shader Twm Visits his Retrospective Exhibition

I approach with hope and reluctance the white-walled
                                        gallery.
A mirror reveals that Soaptruck's wife has trimmed my locks,
Short up the back and yet allowed fullness above the ears,
The way I most dislike it. I enter sideways. Ah, Judge,
My dear chap, you shrink to nothing. Your collar rings
A schoolboy's neck, loose, like an off-white rope. Yes, yes,
My dark boughs do spread out there rather – too stiff and
                                        black,
Rather like dirty hair? My dear Mr Librarian, booze and
                                        heredity
Have made you bloat. When first I knew you you wore wings.

How fascinating that your Aunt Virginia appeared on the
                                        television –
Oh, no, not twice! In lavender and chrome yellow
The Princess Heledd enters, brings in to deafening
Trumpeting, the golden elegance of the young gazelle –
She walks doomed and dappled with sunlight into the
                                        gallery's glare:
In silence the lioness of the future parts the grasses –
Leaps – youth's back is snapped, her dear face chewed off,
Or maybe her left arm gone with gangrene to the elbow
And with already blackened fingers of her right she soothes
The aching stump. Any trace, in that cadaver, of brains, old
                                        lion?
Courage! I look to the buckles of my incredible breastplate,
Loosen in its scabbard my golden blade. You wave to me,
Col., the Hon., Sir, the way you would wave in the
                                        sumptuary laws,
And droit de seigneur. What's art to you, married to that
                                        beautiful
Nit – since you have had your knighthood, your heart attack
And your divorce? No, no, please, Doctor, not another visit,
                                        please;
I know you've peered into all the orifices of the human body
And found the mouth the filthiest – please. Miss
Director of Trickery, you smell sharp like car batteries,
Your skin reminds me of brown something, your nose of
                                        musketry,
An archaic bowsprit. My Lord Bishop, when last I saw God
He was limping, his thigh broken after that wrestling one
                                        night
With you in the Peniel nightclub. Someone must have called
A ducdame – they all flock into the middle of the floor,
Gabbling, turning their backs upon my pictures. Oh, God,
Why have all these to be my brothers and sisters?
Shader leaves.

Roland Mathias
Cae Iago: May Day

Among these arthritic contours
Little atlas and himalaya
Dip down to cwms of glaciered pasture
And stiffen back to the bluff
Of a new rigidity. Most of the old
Walls have fallen, the blackthorn
Splushes have grown out, and each
Of the half enclosures has its
Happy trackway up or on behind
That outburst of rock, beyond
This broken hill. Cock
Pheasants walk these broken
Enclosures, their picking step
Unharrassed. The sheep have their
Winter coats round their ears
And the lambs making play by
Tree roots limber and jump
On each other in the brief
Seconds that sun has
To manoeuvre the clouds away.

It is all new! It is not just
Spring hiding behind snow showers
Or the damson budding again
From its fungused bark. Over
The vanquished summits Ieuan
Appears, his big-wheeled Honda
Trike pursued by sheep, or at
Feeding time rattles a tractor
Down improbable slopes, unbagging
Beet-pulp nuts in trail along
Some shelf of grass, keeping
The hollow bricks of ochred
Minerals topped up. The old

Nomad was right. What has the air
Of cities but obstruction and
The hospital breath of in-fighting?
Up here the men are dead
Who might have argued and the world
Goes on. Snow slants between
This window and Hafotty Ganol's
Ruin across the cwm: the pheasant
Makes his parade: surviving man
Roars up the bounds of his latest kingdom.

John Davies
from Reading the Country

I. Penmon (for Ieuan Wyn)

We left the quarry town still tunnelling.
Roofless, men roofed cities with what they'd found.
What were they looking for? Where the Straits swing
open, it seemed far off, that ripped headland
whose priory also broke new ground.
I'll have your poems translated, I said.

In uncrowded air, a buzzard wavered,
casually tightrope walking. Then flew on
through your language and mine blurred
wordless in the skimming towards Penmon
as if rock's undertow had been washed green
of the faults words still try fathoming, thrown
by the eye over so much space between
us, so much spanning it, above, below.

2. Cwmorthin

It has emptied, that bowl of a valley
hung cracked in Blaenau's draughty rafters, true.
It isn't empty now. Some rework slate.
And the new roads that make all secrets free
send weekend ski jackets glittering through
along paths half a century out of date.

A while back, the mute chapel's disbelief
flared white into graffiti: *Twll tin*
pob Sais and *FWA*. They're fading though.
Trails thicken. It stares like the old chief –
scarfaced, somewhere innocent of wheels
till foraging newcomers cast shadows –
who asked, how many, how many more are...?
and the answer was, "Like the stars".

3. The lost kingdom

"Money," they answered him, the old pair roused
as if by a mansion grown from seed. Young
enough to bend, he tramped farmlight till spined
slopes fattened into valley. The big house
wallowed in shrubbery. He daydreamed. Sprung,
a smoothed passage took him in. Rockshine's
hoard of promises breathed damp where he found
there was no door, so he tapped, hammered, kept
on, hooded in candlesmoke, heard spellbound
his quarryings harvested. They were swept
to a tinkle of glass on the slate wall's
other side. The wall never thinned. Farmland
dreamed him, under its crown of trees. A fall
of light, late on, showed him his ancient hands.

4. An empty cave

it seems, with pools broken open silver

when roofdrops hit. But what has painted
ochre chains on the wall high up, and fur,
is rust. Bolts have orange pelts. Fainter,
moss crawling after light along hacked shelves
halts at a mine shaft. Water has drowned
its plankwalk trodden as if for ever,
floated just out of reach. And bearing down

like outer space is the dense curved weight
on things, given up half-used though not
from choice, on this little globe, dictating
how few remnants survive stopped
ways of life turned suddenly inside out,
the one cave world, and you are in its mouth.

5. Captain John Huws of the *Oriana*

Who? Oh, some ghost here at the marina.
Let's say Davy Jones' locker-cleaner
raised on the local diet of hard rain,
muttering a dying language, Earstrain.
Kill that outboard anyway, get a fix
on lunch. Scramble-up some electronics.

End up as him? Listen, you'd have to be
reefed on sharp memories and all at sea,
give way to God not cabin cruisers, rid
yourself of weekend doldrums, wife and kids,
have sailed tall ships to San Francisco
from Porthmadog or through hell to Rio.

And still be back in time, a bit leaner,
to watch you navigate the marina.

6. The unemployed

Painted white on rough slate at Bethesda:
Bradwyr. It's 1990 but the tale

resurrects itself from chaotic shale
like a wall braced with translation's spars,
words, heart and – No. Just idle surfacings here.
Even lived-through memory's a barrier
my spry uncle must have felt, who clambered
from pit to vicarage and never forgot.
He kept a lone bugler within earshot:
once, clear crossvalley, massed strikers heard
that police under the commanding brow
were coming up. Upward, out. Beneath pews
ran crowded galleries to those he knew
deep-down he could not reach now.

7. Llyn y Gadair (i.m. T.H. Parry-Williams)

Near the freed schoolhouse smoking at Rhyd-ddu,
a slate track still wanders off towards work,
feet thick, over boggy ground. It's a quay
by now: someone has launched into the murk
a Morris Minor where barbed wire, too, dives.
No wonder crowds at Beddgelert choose
a past well-crafted. So little survives,
the plot thins. Why pause? Something, though, moves.

Not two dry quarries crumbling like snow
on a straggle of thirsty conifers,
nor even the lone fisherman towing
his shoal of ripples round the lake. What stirs:
their belonging, stubborn greys, washed browns,
to a dead man's vision not closed down.

8. Old age

Bent over a piled hearth, low on the wall
a blown landscape done in heather, this frame's
too old to straighten. The roof is a sprawled
floor. Casually scratched, look, are not the names
for struggle; more than slate has lost its tongue.

But the window hole keeps studying its sill's
black book and one tree rejoices. Who–? Sun
has questions it will have to ask the hill

or quarry. In the breeze's requiem
for work, shapes reach, wavering from sleep,
the wreck's doorway. It does not know them.

Full of its own clutter, nettles shaking,
what kept the faith so long keeps sheep.
And those, briefly, the new dispersals bring.

9. Thanksgiving day

Climbing where earth once writhed itself a shell
of rock the poor were driven into like nails,
where shadows gather, crowding the levels
to catch the late day home, you heard wind trail

uphill the sincere blasts of a brass band.
A carnival. It crested the main street,
a rogue wave that wind had followed inland,
surprised, then caught ringing on the upbeat.

And rock echoed. It offered the clear site
for remaking, this late, just once only,
somewhere that wouldn't be undermined.

You walked the emptied town. On a still night,
the moon stared down like a face which sees
itself in a mirror with the moon behind.

10. Bits and pieces

Why speak of such things? Because, under news
of the airports' pearly culture eased
through opalescent screens, plain voices say
what joins-up hills is more than just the view.

Because hills blur. Now eyes can't see the trees
for Hollywood, crammed ears turn the way
of the jogger soundproofed against spring.

Dead poets, tracks of the quarrymen, lakes
mining silver – why dabble in such things?
Because the living river of them slakes
now with then. Strongest in ground fractured,
it can flow speechless underground, go slack,
and mistrusts most the fluorescent sea.
But it runs on, pulling-in the country.

Notes: These sonnets were prompted partly by poems translated from the Welsh, the titles
of which have been retained. (A short story by Kate Roberts, 'Old Age', is the exception.)
The poets are: 1: T. Gwynn Jones 2: Gwyn Thomas 3: Iorwerth C. Peate 4: Euros Bowen 5:
W.J. Gruffydd 6: T. Rowland Hughes 7: T.H. Parry-Williams 9: T. Glynne Davies 10: Euros
Bowen. The translations were found in *The Poetry of Wales 1930-1970*, by R. Gerallt Jones
(1974), and *Twentieth Century Welsh Poems* by Joseph Clancy (1982).
In sonnet two, "Twll tin pob Sais" means "arseholes to all Englishmen", and "FWA" stands
for "Free Wales Army". "Bradwyr" ("Traitors") in sonnet six, a reference to strikebreakers,
is a reminder of the 1900-1903 strike at Penrhyn quarries.

Gwyneth Lewis
Dark Ages

Saxons are vertical,
circles we,
hence the mutal hostility.
They climb, we spiral;
who shall be
the better in their eternity?

Curls tend to churls
while ladders rise;
they are legs and we the eyes
that watch the progress of the earls
across the skies
over the clods they patronise.

We are return
but progress they,
roundabout versus motorway.
We borrow but they always own
the deeds of day,
certificates for right of way.

A thane is bright,
no plodder he,
an apex of geometry
that draws the Angles to the heights;
though fantasy
must know the fear of gravity.

The humble are fly
and known the crown
for an O in which a man can drown
or drink his death – such irony
is for the prone
who praise the good they'll never own.

Tony Conran
Lynette Roberts, 1909-1995

LYNETTE ROBERTS DIED at Ferryside on September 26th. She was the last to go of the so-called 'First Flowering' of Anglo-Welsh poetry – David Jones, Dylan Thomas, Idris Davies, Vernon Watkins, Alun Lewis, Glyn Jones – that extraordinarily varied assembly of talent that Keidrych Rhys gathered round his magazine *Wales* in the late thirties and early forties. She only narrowly survived Glyn Jones, who died earlier this year. The giant race before the flood passes into legend.

Of them all, Lynette Roberts's story was the most extraordinary. The details must wait until John Pikoulis publishes his

edition; but she was born of partly Welsh parents and edu-
cated in an Argentine convent and an English boarding
school. She attended classes in woodcarving and textile stud-
ies, but eventually trained as a florist and set up her own
studio in a London attic. She knew many of the writers and
poets of the time, including David Jones, T.S. Eliot, Robert
Graves, Edith Sitwell and Dylan Thomas. She was already
writing poetry, though she had no formal training in litera-
ture; and her work began to find acceptance in magazines.

In 1940 she married Keidrych Rhys, the editor of *Wales*.
From being a rather idiosyncratic groupie on the fringes of
London literary society, she was whisked off to a poverty-
stricken cottage in Llanybri in rural Carmarthenshire, where
she immersed herself in Welsh life – it did not stop the locals
accusing her of being a German spy! It was here, during the
middle years of the war, that she wrote most of the poetry in
her two published volumes, and also a prose book, *Village
Dialect*. They represent only a fraction of her work, some of
which – parts of an autobiography and her correspondence
with Robert Graves while she was helping him gather mate-
rials for *The White Goddess* – appeared in a special edition of
Poetry Wales in 1983. Her two books of poetry *Poems* (1944)
and *Gods with Stainless Ears* (1951) were published by Faber
and Faber. T.S. Eliot admired her work but no subsequent
volumes appeared. The fifties were antipathetic to her kind of
passion and experiment. Her marriage broke up, and after a
few years apparently trying to find a niche in London, she
became a Jehovah's Witness, returned to live in Carmarthen,
and gave up writing poetry.

In Wales she was the only poet of comparable stature not to
benefit from the revival of interest in Anglo-Welsh poetry, the
'Second Flowering' of the sixties and seventies. It was as if
during those years Lynette Roberts was seen largely as an
adjunct to Keidrych Rhys (a much less interesting poet), and
given purely token representation in our anthologies. She had
virtually become a one-poem writer – her invitation to Alun
Lewis to visit her in Llanybri (a fine piece, but not her only one)
was duly trotted out whenever editors had to remember her.

Anglo-Welsh critics and anthologists often disliked Keidrych also, as a person, but they could hardly ignore him as they could his erstwhile wife. It is for ever to the credit of Cary Archard, the then editor of *Poetry Wales,* that he gave nearly a whole number over to her work and its place in literary history.

I met Lynette only once, in her caravan in Hertfordshire in the early fifties. In fact she was the first poet I ever met. She talked about using African drum rhythms and birdsong in poetry – I carried away from our meeting the importance of experiment, of not bowing to dead convention, and the sense that poetry was a sister art to music and painting, and didn't necessarily have to be like 'writing a book'. A sense too that poetry was inter-personal, even if the persons were gods or goddesses; or, even more strenuously demanding of truth, lovers. These insights that she gave me, largely by just being herself rather than by anything she said, have been the corner-stones of my life ever since. In that sense, she was my bardic master; and I do not think I could have had a better one.

I believe that Lynette Roberts wrote some of the best war poetry of the Second World War. 'Crossed and Uncrossed' for instance (a praise-poem for one of her friends), is the finest poem I know about the London blitz (T.S. Eliot's 'Little Gidding' is not primarily about the bombing). Her work is beginning to find readers again. Papers have been given on it in Gregynog seminars and a fine essay on *Gods with Stainless Ears* has appeared in *Critical Quarterly.* I am very happy that the ice-age of neglect is slowly starting to shift, as critics begin to realise what we've been missing.

John Goodby
Ariosto
(after Mandelstam)

It's cold in Europe. In Italy it's dark.
Power, with its sinister barber-hands
thumbs the nape of the neck ... so fling open
a window on the lulled Adriatic, bees

stumbling between musk-roses, the campagna
fidgety with crickets. The sun gongs noon.
Hippogriff prints steam, crescent, in the turf.
Loft the golden dumb-bell of the hourglass.

In the language of cicadas, a woozy blend
of Pushkinian dolour and *sprezzatura,*
incorrigible as ivy, buttonholing,
he fibs heroically about Orlando –

old Aristo, ambassadorial fox,
fern-whorl, sail-stitcher, agave. From the moon
he reported the yellowhammer's song,
on dry land became the instructor of fish.

Soulless, reptile city! You needs sons like those
coarse Ferrara spawned from a jungle and a witch –
harnessed and bitted on a choker rein,
until a red-haired sin lit the wilderness.

Look; the lamb is white against the hill-fold,
a monk jogs by on his ass. The Duke's switzers,
daft with wine and garlic, itch their buboes.
A sausage stall flaps in the shade. A child dozes.

He grins from the balcony, playing the great man.
He addresses oceans, virgin. He clews
us through the maze of chivalric scandal,
dizzy with marvels as we are at our loss.

Richard Poole
The Millennium Can Kiss My Arse

Okay, let's cut the crap before you split.
2000's coming: this is really it.
The planet's fucked, it isn't worth a shit.

It's wobbling through the stupid universe
To nowhere in particular, or worse.
At night it's like an interstellar hearse.

We're molecules in transit till we die –
Electrons, protons, quarks. No ponce knows why.
We're mostly holes. We're talking raspberry pie.

I'm out of smokes. I'm broke. I'm on the dole,
Hemmed in by herpes, AIDS and Helmut Kohl.
The ozone layer's one big fucking hole.

The climate's freaked out on an acid trip.
Icebergs are ice-cubes. If you dare to strip,
The sunshine nukes you like a micro chip.

The Honda's wrecked. The telly's repossessed.
The cat's dead and Fiona's lost a breast.
The bog's blocked. Check – Fiona's flown the nest

Back to her bloody mother up in Stoke –
To bourgeois comforts, Bensons, rum and Coke.
I bet some bastard's giving her a poke.

The market rules, the earth's a shopping mall.
The bankers have us by the balls, old pal.
They'd lend their sisters to a cannibal.

Philosophy's bollocks. God was just a con.
Plato's for dickheads. Zen's for Uncle John.
Existentialism's wank now Sartre's gone.

Sweet Jesus save us from the *á la mode* –
The blacks and queers, the feminists in woad.
Thank Christ Post-modernism's shot its load.

Politics kill me. Socialists are nerds.
The Libs are glib. Conservatives are turds.
Their mouths drop open, and you drown in words.

The world's jam-packed with nutters, guys with guns.
They've brains the size of peas and balls like buns.
They're flogging drugs to every mother's sons.

Truth, like the green belt's getting pretty sparse.
The heat is on the take, the law's a farce
And every judge's head is up his arse.

The monarchy's a soap for brain-dead mums
Whose brats crash stolen cars in rotting slums
Or mince round London, living off their bums.

The globe's an orange that a nipper nicked,
A cricket ball the Paki quicks unpicked,
A dozy turnip Vinny Jones miskicked.

Jason's on crack. Electra's up the spout.
Her brain's jammed in her womb and can't get out.
And who's she shacked up with? Some City lout.

Rent's overdue, the flat looks like a tip.
The sofa's sinking like a battleship.
If I'd the energy, I'd up and skip.

So why not top myself – get out of it,
Clock off, kiss concrete, do a body flit,
Deploy the instant life-disposal kit?

To lay it out for you, I'm scared to die –
To wink out like a red-hot-pokered eye.
I'm still here, girls. And now you all know why.

Mike Jenkins
from Rebel Voices

1. Songs In My Head
    for A.B.

There are no better tickets
than these gifts you give
these rattling boxes
passed like illicit substances
at our occasional booze-ups.

I want to praise now
long before any elegy
your studiously penned
funny and angry titles
THIS TAPE KILLS 99%
OF ALL FASCISTS DEAD
or the NOT WHAT IT READS one:
you should've had a band
just for the covers alone.

Journeys unwind: the brown path,
the shining rails, the thin
road leading away
to Africa or Ireland
obscure names like places
only you discover,
Marxman, Best Shot, Tarika:
villages into towns into countries.

The music of your recordings
the passports never stamped
the borders always open:
songs in my head flying.

2. Through Black Rain

for Tim Richards

If, on a wet Thursday evening
in the middle of a dark December
at a dead-end valley institute
(due to be closed down)
you came to talk to a meeting
and only two turned up
(one of them the caretaker!) –
you'd still speak with summit passion,
you'd still leave with optimism
not needing 10 pints of whoosh
to believe in that revolutionary
change from without and within.

We're brothers of these notions
yet we joke about campaigns:
buckets of lime and pasted posters,
Che Guevaras on traffic islands,
police in courts to sit you down
and M.P.'s surgeries with no prescriptions.
Towards the mountain, your many talents
are paths and each direction
brings a challenge: arrêtes
and chasms. You'd never follow,
you'd be armed with a torch
deaf to thunder, knowing
we'd climb through black rain
to breathe clear for the first time,
at the top your memorial inscribed
THE STRUGGLE HAS JUST BEGUN.

Peter Finch
The Student House

We arrive through thin snow to
my son's student house where
no one has been for three weeks.
The ice has turned the air to knives.
I find a ketchup-smeared plate
frozen at 45° in the unemptied
kitchen sink. A river of lager
cans flows down the hall.
As I stamp into the lounge
keeping my feet alive the ghosts
of dust come up around me like
children. The stains across the
sofa look like someone has died.
Amid the wrappers and old news
washing against the skirting I
spot the letter I sent up six months
back. It's up to you, I wrote,
you are on your own now,
no one can do this for you,
something like that.
He enters the room in his ripped
jeans and shrunken sweat-shirt
fingers locked in his arm-pits.
Do we clear this place? Can't be bothered,
the energy has been
frozen out of us. He hands
me the torch. I go to the basement
to see if I can fix the boiler, no
longer in charge but still trying,
the fallen king. I light the pilot
and the heat comes back,
a kind of love, pressing us softly
as we stand saying goodbye
amid the junk mail in the hall.

M. Wynn Thomas
"All lenient muscles tensed":
The Poetry of Roland Mathias

"A FOOL'S MOUTH is his destruction, and his lips are the snare of his soul... Death and life are in the power of the tongue ... Whoso keepeth his mouth and his tongue keepeth his soul from troubles." In its awesome concern with the ethics of utterance, the Book of Proverbs provides us with an example of the kind of spiritually fraught poetics that may, for believers, be implicit in the Bible's gloss on the use and abuse of language. From Herbert to Hopkins there were poets who racked not so much their minds as their very souls before daring to commit their words to paper to trouble posterity. Their spiritual next of kin in our own times include Paul Celan and Geoffrey Hill, writers traumatised by the way "the tongue's atrocities" became unutterably evident in the Holocaust.

That in Wales we have in R.S. Thomas a major writer of this anguished kind is widely recognized. What is not appreciated is that in Roland Mathias, his exact contemporary, we have another of like spirit although not of comparable stature. Not only may his eight or so volumes of poetry seem slight when weighed against the sheer bulk and intellectual muscle of Thomas's collected work, they are also over-shadowed by Mathias's own outstanding achievements as editor, critic, and literary historian. And the poems seem, in any case, almost to invite impatient dismissal as the mere by-product of Mathias's professional career as pedagogue and intellectual. The vocabulary can be arcane, the learning archaic, the syntax tangled. There may indeed be little incentive to continue reading, unless perchance one stumbles on some such moving, lucid passage as the following, with which he concludes his elegy for his mother:

> I have no prayers like hers, that sprang
> Hard from the laid-down rock, but now,
> All lenient muscles tensed, I'll practise long

After dark, if she remember too.

Like this passage, all Mathias's poetry starts from a con-
vinced sense of moral and spiritual shortcomings – those
endemic to a fallen humanity, those characteristic of his own
complaisant times, and those personal to himself.
Permanently fearful of moral laxity, of sinful self-indulgence
(he has ruefully admitted in interview to an ingrained senti-
mentality), Mathias responds to the blandishments of
language by treating it with a kind of punishing, and self-
punishing, sensual severity. Nervously alive to the static
electricity lurking in the nap of words, he handles them with
circumspection, of which his poetry's guarded syntax is the
outward and visible sign. Fully to appreciate it one needs to
reflect on the ethics of the sentence, and on the spiritual ide-
ology inscribed in grammatical structures. Seeking to pick his
scrupulous way past the plain lies of seductive rhetoric,
Mathias tends to advance his thinking not in straight lines but
zigzag as a knight manoeuvres in chess. He thus deliberately
cramps his style in order to ensure that moral conscience
keeps pace with verbal fluency, and consequently some of his
lines are almost prickly with integrity. The resulting embran-
gled poetry could be described as modern puritan baroque,
its harsh music echoing what is for Mathias the only durable
song of the lapsarian earth:

> Patently
> It is the grasshoppers I
> Must listen to, as they intersperse
> A hard leg-music with mad
> Travels from tussock to bleaker
> Tuft, to broken stick or random
> Protuberant stone.

This 'hard leg-music', fitting accompaniment to
mankind's errant and erratic ways, is to be heard in several of
the most powerful English language poems published in
Wales since the war; but Mathias's astringently mannered
writing has also not infrequently displayed the weaknesses of
its strengths. The tensing of lenient muscles can sometimes

result in painful cramps and verbal spasms; a magisterial dis-
taste for all things shoddy can degenerate into merely
schoolmasterly disapproval; moral rigour can begin to sound
disconcertingly like prissiness; the sustained dialogue with
history may seem no more than the meanderings of a man-
darin antiquarian. These are not, of course, failings in the
man but rather the effect of periodic failures of his style, and
since at its best that style unselfconsciously creates an effect
of humbling moral integrity, it is in related terms – more
moral than aesthetic – that one tends to register the short-
comings of his poetry.

The successes of that poetry, however, are as singular in
kind as they are notable in quality. Mathias's strenuous
tongue (to misappropriate Keats's phrase) has for example
given us 'Testament', 'Porth Cwyfan', 'Brechfa Chapel' and
'Burning Brambles', and the depth of his talent became fully
evident when he published his selected poems in 1983, as he
approached his seventieth birthday. The stroke he suffered a
few years later seemed to have brought his admirably pro-
ductive life as a writer to a permanent halt, but his lifelong
determination never to capitulate to weakness, either of mind
or of body, reasserted itself, this time in the form of a strug-
gle to overcome his disabilities, and the publication of *A Field
at Vallorcines* a year ago was indeed a triumph of the spirit.

The volume is all the more a triumph in that so many of
the poems (albeit predating Mathias's stroke in many cases)
are of vintage calibre, and it is all the more moving in that
from the very outset the experience of ageing is factored into
the writing by various unaffected means. The very first
poem, 'Onset of Winter', serves in this respect as prologue to
the whole, concerned as it is with the way the cold lays
deathly claim to a landscape, threatening to chill faith itself to
the very marrow. That, however, is not the end of the story
because

> ...for all the miss
> In the steady beat
> Of the walking blood
> Stopped at the bark

The lamed man keeps his heat
Aware, like the cold, shut clod,
An ancienter oath will answer this.

That use of "oath" is in part faith's robust response in kind
to the first stanza, where early snow was heard to "swear",
with a crude swagger, that winter would soon arrive to make
good its threat to annihilate all life. But the phrase "ancienter
oath" also has the effect of transposing the argument
between life and death into a decisively different key, since in
this context "oath" additionally signifies a solemn undertak-
ing, the binding promise of life's eternal triumph over death
made by the One whose presence in these concluding lines is
all the more powerful for being left unspoken, as "clod" is
allowed to rhyme silently with "God". Metaphysical turns of
wit and sleights of tone of this kind have always been a fea-
ture of Mathias's writing, but this is one of those telling
occasions where they are seen to originate in the knot of feel-
ings associated with his deep personal faith.

In *A Field at Vallorcines* that faith is tested by a world of
loss. "Must I ghost them downward" Mathias wonders in his
beautiful poem 'Signal'. Even as the leaves of the wisteria fall
around him, he fails either to anticipate their fall or to catch
them in the very act. Position himself as he will, "Their first
take-off / Is secret", and never glimpsed save out of the very
corner of his eye. Thus do we often fail to notice, even in
those we know well, the first decisive signs of the gravitational
pull of death. And once those are made apparent, then, as
Mathias's lovely phrase about "ghost[ing] them downward"
suggests, we often become witnesses helpless as spectres to
prevent the terminal declensions of the flesh. Moreover, as
the phrase further implies, in that decline we sense the
ghostly presence of our own, as young Margaret, in
Hopkins's celebrated poem about 'Spring and Fall', insensi-
bly mourned for herself as she grieved "over Golden Grove
unleaving".

Mathias's two elegies to his mother provide touching
examples, in *A Field at Vallorcines*, of another kind of "ghost-
ing downward" that is such a significant feature of this

volume. In its opening speculation about whether there is "a bearing to this spot" from his mother's resting place in the next world, 'Aber' encapsulates one of Mathias's abiding concerns – the concern to take his own bearings in life through carefully considered reference to, and acknowledgement of, those who have passed this way before. So, in 'Expiation', he seeks to make a kind of amends to a grandfather he feels he has previously slighted in print, because "to deny / The dead a voice is to falter / In justice." Enfolded in such phrasing is Mathias's belief in the obligation to develop a responsible historical imagination, one that can appreciate the deep human import (i.e. moral legacy) of materials even from the remote, legendary past. In 'Cynog' he wonders from which clifftop, and into which of two possible streams, was the sixth century Breconshire saint hurled to his death by Irish raiders, because for the searcher what is "At stake is benison / Not history". Mathias strongly feels that places have an aura, that they are numinous with their past, and that present lives are everywhere lived in the light of a prehistory of which they may all too often be unaware but under whose silent judgement they nevertheless, unknowingly, sit.

Indeed, for Mathias the present is to be understood as bound to the past by a complex "entail of dependence", as Burke put it, the moral terms of which have repeatedly been explored in his poetry through a process of interrogation as fierce as Jacob's wrestling with the angel. For this purpose, Mathias – the historian agonistes – has notoriously chosen to employ a wrenched syntax and an archaic language sometimes resembling a pastiche of Browning's pastiche of the vernacular of past times. But this mode of writing has its undeniable, highly idiosyncratic successes, as in 'The Steward's Letter', a poem "closely based on a letter written by Lord Burghley's steward" at the end of the sixteenth century. It concerns the stratagems by which the Cecil family acquired a mansion in the Welsh marches, and the missive's language – muscular, yet florid with courtesy – is instinct with equivocation and duplicity, just as its tone is a fascinating mixture of deference and insolence.

Also evident in the crypto-Elizabethan English of 'The Steward's Letter' is Mathias's relish for thickly textured discourse. He loves it when words sound so chunky that they seem to stand proud off the page like Braille, hence in part the enlistment of words like "chalybeate", "gamboge", "frowsty", "skullhead", "flummoxed". These are, one might say, words that are not afraid to stand up and be counted. When he describes Cynog's "bulking robe" he could as well be describing his own practice of filling out meaning by bestowing sharply physical presence on abstract qualities or fleeting phenomena (the "blunt faces" of monks; a tern's "blade-bone / Cleaving the wavelets' / Interface"; "these spasms of wittering" that characterise sanderlings; Ronan's "few spindle-stick / Tries to sharpen / Thoughts"). Implicit in such a practice is Mathias's reluctance to sunder flesh from mind or spirit. His is a world in which all things, and all people, body forth what they most truly and intimately are, revealing their inner moral being in their physical bearing and demeanour. That is why he is an instinctive allegorist, one of the tribe of Bunyan for whom moral attributes have their own tell-tale body language, and the corporeal realm bears everywhere the marks of the great moral struggle of which existence itself essentially consists.

In 'Brechfa Chapel' Mathias warned severely that "Each on his own must stand and conjure / The strong remembered words, the unanswerable / Texts against chaos." Couched as they are in terms of strength and struggle, his ethics and poetics alike take on a markedly gendered character. He comes across as a very "masculine" writer, and nowhere is this more arrestingly evident than in the poem which is, perhaps, the single most notable achievement in *A Field at Vallorcines*. 'The Path to Fontana Amorosa' records – in a form strongly reminiscent of the old allegorical topos of the bivium – a northern puritan male's ambivalent response to the "feminized" landscape of ancient Mediterranean cult and culture. Setting out on the path to the Baths of Aphrodite, in Cyprus, Mathias (although universalizing and emblematizing the experience by attributing it simply to the second person singular – "you") uneasily allows himself to be seduced by the lushness of the landscape in this, "the white goddess's country". Wantoning in abundance, the whole coastline, as "reckless" as it is "magical", seems to beckon him towards "the spring / Where the gush is all women's abandon". However, within this sensuous Eden there lurks a serpent, a snake that has turned an amorous lizard into a corpse lying bloated on the path. Morally sobered by the sight, Mathias is recalled to his senses, and to a minatory awareness of the history of this place. For if it is, on one "reading" of its past, the legendary haunt of Aphrodite, it is also, on another such "reading", the site of the ancient and long since extinct city of Marion:

> Eucalyptus
> Trees, a grove half skirted with bamboo eyots
> Cursed in with gravel and sea-water,
> Quiver where Marion was. That speaking grave
> For all you know despairs with its words
> Awash.

Chaos has, then, prevailed against whatever strong, remembered words the ancient city of Marion had to offer, but Mathias implicitly honours the spirit of those words, and thus reaffirms the realm of order, when he chooses not to proceed to Aphrodite's baths. Cautioned by death, he (although still to the end concealed by the impersonal, or omnipersonal, "you") recovers his prudence and is able to withstand the dangerous solicitations of the extravagant flesh.

The poem is, of course, grounded in Mathias's sophisticated awareness of the host of moral and literary conventions that his text is heir to. Indeed, it would be perfectly possible to treat it in richly intertextual terms, by considering the ways in which meanings are produced through implicit references to works by Graves, Spenser, Bunyan and so on. But equally significant are the gendered terms in which Mathias constructs his moral geography. The female is unmistakably treated as representing the ambivalent realm of moral transgression – ambivalent because its dangers are proportionate to its promise of a different order, or an enhanced dimension, of experience (involving artistic achievement as well as personal fulfilment). And in the light of this it becomes noticeable how, in his second elegy for his mother, Mathias's greatest compliment to her is to represent her in terms of a masculine image. Rather than describe her as a home-maker, he recalls how "for thirty-nine narrowing years / My mother it was kept the house / Squared at its peers." Such a designation goes with his (ambivalent?) reflection that his parents' home, although named "Tŷ Clyd" ("Cosy House") was anything but that in moral reality:

> Cosy was rarely its state
> Over decades of waiting when *clyd*
> White-lettered the gate.
> Principled rather, two storeys of deeds
> Slapped on word, a house with all chance
>   crusades
> Abandoned, a crux of definitive shades
> Attacking the quiet.

One might suggest that it is some such house as this – ambivalently characterized as bleak, straitened, but impressively "principled" – that Mathias has striven to build through his own life, just as he has striven to keep the word "clyd"/cosy out of the text he has written to accompany that life. And one might further surmise that some such figure as that which he makes of his mother in this elegy has served as a kind of muse of his poetry – equal but opposite in power to Graves's white goddess. 'The Path to Fontana Amorosa' concludes with a reaffirmation of Mathias's faithful service to that salvific muse, but not before he has feelingfully questioned the terms of such service. Just for a moment, he entertains the possibility that what he has regarded as the preconditions of moral strength may be no more than the expression of psychological weakness; that he has stuck to the straight and narrow only because he is afraid of death, afraid of risk, afraid of the unruly sprawl of the senses, afraid of the "female". Likewise, his tribute to his mother is humanly strengthened, as poetry, by the mere possibility allowed for in the elegy's phrasing that her particular kind of strength was purchased at a price, at the cost of a lack of nurturing warmth, of a curtailment of the "feminine" virtues.

The proper conditions for spiritual probity are again considered in 'Ronan', the story of an early Breton saint who lived a hermit's life. The bulk of the poem turns on the contrast between Ronan's solitary cave dwelling ("The bare hill-top was / A discipline / Struck // Above") and the swarmingly sinful life in the valley below:

> It was word
> Of such commonwealth
>   Kept
> Ronan
>   Abhorrent in his cave
> Rapt in the mien
> Of saint, an opinion
>   That love was untouchable
> Save for the one
>   Alone in the cosmos.

Mathias's disapproval of such moral egotism is unmistakable, and is no doubt all the stronger for his understanding that there are Ronanesque tendencies in his own nature. He has to struggle to keep his distaste for contemporary life within proper bounds, and in his poetry this struggle takes the form of a flinching from any signs of spiritual pride in his own bearing towards the world. These reactions are interwoven in 'Jazz Festival', where he begins by testily objecting to the "rumpus / In the small hours of the afternoon" (his underlying fear of Circean revelry also emerging in his characterizing of the event as viscerally primitive as "the vainglorious shapes of riot / Which the shuffling out-island slaves / Would put on when Picton had / The reins in Trinidad") before concluding that the "vexed bass", which is all the sound the ear can detect as it sets protective distance between itself and the town, is a humbling reminder of the pulse of the fallen flesh which is common both to the "rioters" and to himself.

"What I am trying to say / Looks foolish, doesn't it",

reflects Mathias at the beginning of 'Jazz Festival', "With all this noise going on?" Part of the poignancy and power of *A Field at Vallorcines* is the feeling it generates of one who has grown old in the service of values and beliefs that the world has increasingly held to be foolish. The dignity and consequentiality of Mathias's achievement as a poet is, however, rooted in his unwavering determination to make poetry rhyme with principle. As a result his work at its best possesses those inestimable qualities he identifies in the concluding lines of 'A Field at Vallorcines':

> The run down the gorge to the frontier, the silent
>   place
>
> We peered at this morning with so little
> In mind, will be full of jerks and slowings
>
> Like the blind climb up. But the station has grace.
>   It has borne
>
> The faces of doubts, the comings and goings
> Of millions. We shall stand there solid in
> The goodly counsel with which a world back we
>   set out.

Mike Jenkins
Merthyr People
(for Steve Phillips, photographer)

Waltzing Eyes

She's framed by the Zimmer, knits her arthritic fingers into
    each other, the crotchety texture of her pain.
The present is a tea-cup (no saucer), the stump of a candle,
    an egg-cup full of pins.
Further along the mantelpiece the dice are all on one, a photo
    of her grandchildren burnt white by her cataracts.
It becomes darker: her hubby's trophy, his leather-bound portraits a modest library.

Her skin is falling. At her feet are neatly-chopped logs. If she
   should rub her bones much harder, then a spark…
There's smoke from her grey hair. If only her flesh were
   grained like wood.
Behind her shoulders the plant has turned to soot.
You won't see her waltzing eyes till the flames begin.

Wolf-Hour

It's wolf-hour in the precinct: pack of dogs, pack of boys.
The mirror can't be seen. They reflect and swop features,
triads with sharpened fangs.

Leaders face nose to snout, staring each other out.

Three concrete blocks where winners would stand to
receive a battered coke-can cup.

The dogs are more patient: paw-leafed pavingstones are
their horizons.

The boys have blurry feet. One jerks in incredible contor-
tions, head taking off over the binned estate.

Hip-hop away, their leader's flung a can — 'Fuckin mangy
strays! Don' shit yer!' His hair thick as an alsatian's coat.

It's wolf-hour in the precinct: the Shop Boys lurk in the
background, from a ridge of reputation. Night comes, they'll
snap up and pocket the silver moon.

Shadow Without Sun

Perched on a black and white pillar, call him 'Piggy', he
doesn't care. His head's two storeys above his sister.

His knee jabbers for him, saying – 'I'm loud 'n' dirty, I'm
bloody mucky, open t' the air.'

Arms folded, captain of a team of one, holding the match
ball, his cheeks blown up.

He's casting a shadow without the sun. She's in it, clutch-
ing her check skirt in case the wind… Her hair's the shine of
a plastic bucket.

Her face conceals a window. His hair is curtained, tousled,
already drawn.

Sheenagh Pugh
Unkindness

A dead man is so like to a man sleeping,
whispered the professor, when she laid eyes
on the gentle face a peat-spade turned over
in Tollund bog. The centuries-old unkindness

that buried him there had only marked his brow
with little furrows, like a man's in a dream.
He lay relaxed on his side. She almost thought
she could have shaken his shoulder and woken him.

So I feel, seeing you lie, somewhat stiffer
than usual, so that lifting your slight weight
is no such easy matter. I can't notice
anything missing: no, not even the light

of wit in your open eyes. There is just the stiffness,
and a little crust of dried blood at the mouth,
and is that any reason to leave a kind companion
alone for an iron age in the black earth?

Alun Rees
The Cabbages of Maidanek

At Maidanek they killed the Jews
and turned them into soups and stews.

First they were stripped and showered. Then
into delousing rooms, and when

down through the vents came cyanide
like a blue snowfall, the Jews died.

They sold the dentures off for cash
and burned the bones for fertile ash,

and laid that ash upon a field
and fed the camp upon its yield.

Enriched with Jewish bones and toil,
cabbages rose from Jewish soil,

their leaves all green with growing's tones,
their veins as strong and white as bones.

But did the blue-eyed Aryan troops
know they were eating kosher soups?

Or realise that they, perforce,
grew steadily Jewish course by course?

It was so efficient, well designed:
each death was stamped and sealed and signed.

Each Jew was killed in triplicate,
then resurrected on a plate.

A million and a half were killed:
oh, what a shame if the soup were spilled

to go to waste down some dark drain
and make their sacrifice in vain.

And how to understand? Don't try:
just eat your cabbage up, and cry.

T.H. Jones
Portsmouth at Night: 'Hostilites Only' Rating

Ghosted with sailors, the sleeping city
Waits by the water for an admiral
To take her out to sea. Down the long decks
That are her streets I hear the carol
Of dead marines and (gallant) snotty midshipmen
Ruffle the rigging of the *Victory.*
The sea-wind carrying ecstasies of rum
Forbids me to indulge in idle pity
For those who've sailed from here to a long sleep
Where mermaids give them cold and coral welcome.
The Pompey chimes ring out over seven seas.
Portsmouth is pointed for a long commission.
I am a sailor and on watch again.
And as I walk these admiralty streets,
I make a prayer for Pompey's able seamen:
Lord, on the day when earth your judgement meets,
Remember that I once was one of these.

(19 June, 1957)

John Powell Ward
She Wrote to Me

one

Thirteen Canada-geese flew over
But one seemed to split, which thus made
Fourteen. Every night my dream
Was of being pinned to a ledge,

Whether office-block or sheer cliff,
And the vertical height made my bowel
Sag, and there was no centre of gravity
Left for me. On the new mobile phone

I tried to call up, them to hoist me up
But the sound went down, pulling my
Eyeballs after it. Gorgeous red
Trees and fields lay calmly

Before us and then turned green.
Oh that the earth could again be green.
Nevermore. The flat spin of the stars
Returned and that was all my grace.

two

I bought a flat, near the cathedral walls
Whose moat was a kind of ring-road now
For all these days. There was no coal fire,
So we walked and walked, breathing

The pasture's air, the deep hang-glider
Wafting across like a moth to burnish his song.
Into the snow the handpicked tourists marched,
Playing their disks and paying their bills,

The President's term still not up. But
Across the sea, where the rugby games were played,
A huge bird, a colossal eagle soared,
And I named it 'Cobalt Blue' for itself,

There being no pair, whereby it might seed
A further again. Maybe the furniture knew,
Or the tall radio towers that grew like trees,
Shedding their bulletins like autumn leaves.

three

After the night, when the new pen was delivered,
I made a box for paints, and kept the song
In a plastic wrapper, as the gardening manuals
Decreed. There was simply no time,

The years had sprinted away, round the last bend,
And the Jumbo's gold had climbed its stair
Up to that stratosphere where Plato worked,
Filling his diary, having his chocolate drink

At eleven. Into the Gothic church
The cavalry rode, their liveries green
As the new-tipped grasses built on Easter day.
A cabinet meeting broke up, order

Maintained as was its womanly wont,
For these are the days, when everything
Is decided once and for all, the electronic
Machine is might, and tells, and is invisible.

four

Delightfully the T-shirt and the jeans
Swing on the line and show their subtle arts
Caressing the flesh they espouse. Only a man
Going skywards in an elevator-express

Could doubt the instants of the coffee bean,
The unbought share, the caravan where
The great waves break and swim breathlessly
To the sand. A giraffe appeared at that

Point, slowly gyrating its huge
Opinions and then dodged gracefully away.
A serpent slid back down its tube, which
It fitted exactly. My domestic camera

Quietly advises me not to say a word,
In case some solicitor hears, and starts
To trapeze, as people will when happiness
Jumps unexpectedly, on the new-mown grass.

five

We need a word for *God* and there isn't one.
So maybe quiet is real, or the very sound
Of grass scraping on sand, billowing the air's
Pollution we've come to love and not unmake.

Jesus the bit that died, his blood trickling
As from someone killed in a crash, the driver mad
With fast-lane speed, his sperm shot
From an overwrought mind where big cats slugged

In outer space, that outer, outer space,
Where science pours its neutralizing hopes,
Announcing in print the crazy possibilities
No one chose and no one else would have known,

The letters all sent in pillar-box red
To destinations we don't even know are there.
Others turned into mice, dogs into men,
The creation blazoned with bread, chance and dream.

six

The gold they valued, longer lasting than truth,
Unrusting like iron, unbending like lead,
Beautiful as urine or the spring primrose,
Where I carved a destroying meat and ate

My fill. Even the tortoise can't overturn
In its shell, and then go right side up
Like a kayak used in fitness sports.
The screens danced to the conductor,

The announcer rattled the evening facts
While with his hidden left hand
Reached to the side for the curdled drink
In which the mixing girl had put more gin

Than an unbuilt reservoir intended for the rain
We let slip to the seaside, year by year
Still cleaning our priceless teeth, those
Exquisite gems, through which to tell our hearts.

seven

She wrote to me, I knew that hand.
Spindly and sweet, like a child's favourite sky.
At the motorway halt we had soup, and kept
All the free coupons, my bank so grateful, while

Fourteen men, each the line of a sonnet, lit
Their taboo nicotine and started their trek
Up the cold glacial slopes. Their green
Coats mirrored the last constellations

The space-probe would ever reach. Crying,
The women lay on the ground, a black
Baby was born and it shall never die. Frogs,
Jumping into the pond, were so persuasive

In how to swim for the best, not to mind
Their lot or imagine that becoming princes
Would pay off the mortgage or clean
The mess from the hills, of work and love.

eight

The vehicles drove to the nub, a centripetal
Starfish, cheering the heart. When they returned
It was dusk, and people toasted their scones
On specially-heated air. A schoolgirl ran

Across the park to her door at this time,
Chased of course, but no one else would

Have known her name's derivation, or that
It was etched on silver in her purse,

A grandma's gift. Blue the huge colour,
Snow the moment that stayed, and a wounded man,
Rebelling against the arms a government
Sent, stared at the poppies which grew

On his legs and chest. Even the roundabout spun,
But the tune it played on that cranky old
Machine gave out more teams than a dictionary,
Hung on the garden tree for a thousand years.

Samantha Wynne-Rhydderch
Bridal Suite Variations

Christ, here they come again, the arm twisters
and the chain smokers, remembering their lines
halfway through: the same pressed tails
and hatbands that have bowed before
generations of lenses. Richard trips
out of the hedge with his usual spliff.
All the best men hunched like embarrassed
ghosts in the last pew, a handful of decades
between them. Finally, the daughters
of the Hesperides looking up at the stained glass
faces, solemn as the vicar's magenta robe.

Enter the sailor off left in his wet
Muriel, I love you more than the tide
felt hat, perfecting his speech
inside the drowned towers where I have cried
during the hymned interval of rings
and seen your eyes at dead of night
and all the best men stare because

when the bells toll from the wrecked ships
they know what happens if you don't.

At the toast to the groom, the wreck
of the *Bronwen* rises moaning
along the seabed. The figurehead
on her prow bites the sand,
Alice in her blue velvet dress,
her hands full of barnacles,
an anchor through her breast.

Gwyneth Lewis
The Mind Museum

I *The Museum Curator Greets the Dawn*

At nine, I switch on our TV dawn:
the South Wales Transport video game;

Treasures from our Archive (on the blink)
showing some shipwrecks before going blank;

a potted history of the mineral trade
with dotted lines across the world;

and then, my favourite, a timelapse tide
breathing water in weather-wide

and out of the harbour. And then I switch
on haulage engines for the delight

of watching the piston elbows rise and fall.
Precision makes work as musical

as any orchestra. Then I stand
on the model bridge and understand

a museum's museum is being alive.
Quiet please, madam. Yes, we close at five.

II *History Lesson*

Time was they walked on water dry
so full of ships were the teeming docks.
We dream in video what they lived by day.

Masts bobbed like crosses at a crowded quay,
sank from sight inside the gurgling lock.
Time was they walked on water dry.

Men had to travel for a fireman's pay,
they sweated bullets but enjoyed the crack.
We dream in video what they lived by day.

Murmansk, Osaka, Paraguay:
the girls they met there call them back...
Time was they walked on water dry,

met Welshmen everywhere, and lay
by stanchions up some Godforsaken creeks.
We dream in video what they lived by day.

Back home in Cardiff, hear the halyards play
sweet music when the winds fall slack.
Time was they walked on water dry.
We dream in video what they lived by day.

III *Website Future*

No need for me once we're on the net,
are a wave to be surfed on, have gone world-wide.
No awkward engines to curate
but templates which never knew a tide.

And if TV signals are never lost
but flare round the world until a mind

receives them, then surely this e-mail will last
much longer than paper. Fast-forward, rewind

are history. Let the servers serve
their megabyte karma in encoded air.
Long live the roll of the mouse, the curve
of choices made when I won't be here.

Then nobody'll tell us where we've just been
but we'll make our own history, piece by piece,
be free to improvise and glean
our version, far from chronicle police.

But on monitors the bands of rain
sweep in, interference on our charts.
Remember the real matters more than the known.
Unforecast snow falls softly in our hearts.

IV *Communications*

I phoned him from a standing stone
to prove to him that I was still there.
And I was worshipful:
granite, horizon, message, air.

I called him from a holy well
hoping for miracles, a cure.
My prayers cost dearly in time
and candles. But he didn't care.

I dialled via satellite.
I needed an answer to my despair.
I got it. *Sorry, we can't connect you.*
Please try again later. Nobody here.

V *On Duty*

First things first: the Crossword of the Day,
which I do while showing visitors the way.

I'm paid for boredom and the tide
of non-events on which I ride.

We're waiting to hear about our jobs.
Six across could be the *Ace of Spades*.

What would I curate if I had to leave?
These mud flats? *Anagram: Reprieve.*

The open handbag of a screaming gull?
The passing clouds? *Fifteen is Dull.*

The crossword setter, my anonymous friend
gives me clues to my unknown mind.

These are snakes and ladders you'll never climb
or follow to anywhere. Last word is *Time.*

VI *Night Galleries*

Maybe today they'll change the tapes!
It's the same old stories – first there was steam,
steel, then depression, then developed bay –
stories so fixed I can never say
more than they let me. At night I dream

these galleries shift. We open screens,
show new exhibits. The best one's my heart
in a glass case and it switches on
and off like a light bulb. This intimate room
is floodlit, is a work of art. Stop, start. Stop, start. Stop,
start.

Lynette Roberts

Love is an Outlaw

Love is an outlaw that cannot be held
Within the small confines and laws of man;
Rather it will turn, as a planet can,
Man upside down, like a first line fabled
In a notebook lightly pencilled upon
To change his sense of direction. Dimpled
Wisely like an unbridled child, love is pebbled
With smooth water and myths: a glazed swan
Shadowed in reeds: a ray of light waylaid
On swiftly moving motes. Wholesome love attends
Its own shape, warm and shining. The man who tends
The herds and street lamps symbols of its trade:
It is pacing Genesis on two legs
Dispossessing man who unapparelled begs.

Circe: The Falcon

I wish I was a bird again,
To fill his sight with golden eyes,
To draw him out into the Bay
And be his falcon for a day.

I wish to circle his dark form,
As love, invisibly go by,
Fly in, around his savage rocks
That hide our timbered nest and flocks.

I wish to free his mind of fear,
Float bells and shells upon the air,
To see his boat rejoice with spray
And hear him sing to clouds that stray.

But I am just an old grey crone,
Whose feathers are but dusty bone,
He's gone away far out of sight
And left me in the Bay's bleak light.

Sheenagh Pugh

Elegy

for the books lost in the fire at the Canton Library, Cardiff 1997

William Thomas, schoolmaster, your voice,
those catty, irascible, eighteenth-century diaries
where your neighbours lived on, ears burning, you'd
                                        have known
what he was, the malignant dullard whose only light
came from his matches: you'd have called him a 'crot'.

Barbara Palmer, her life: kings and rope-dancers,
money and love scattering like light,
there's more where that came from, nightly invading
Pepys's delighted dreams: you chose some cads,
but never one without any wit.

The red *Handmaid*, banned from reading tales,
writing her own. Milton: *as good kill
a man, as a good book*; knowing that words
are the witness to our share in reason,
that to hate words is to hate the light.

Worldmakers, manmakers, more god than God,
your creatures live for ever, you can shape
Troy or Ankh-Morpork, you light the clay.
You could make that clod, if you had a mind to,
but he, having none, could make nothing.

He'd only come to steal the computers;
waiting for a getaway van

that never showed. So why set light
to the building – frustration, pique,
tedium, something else he couldn't spell?

I think he stood here, sensing all around
the voices of thought and fancy, the fluent voices
of folk who could string sentences together,
and dimly he felt light crowding in,
threatening, defining his limits,

so he got rid of it: lit a fire
to put out light. Weeks later, workmen
in the blackened shell are still coughing ash,
while the old folk hang round the door,
thinking of warmth, gossip, newspapers.

May he end up in hell, seeing nothing
but your names in print, hearing only words
of grace and wisdom, the glittering spell
of your grammar, knowing his own measure,
charred, shrivelled, eyes burned out with light.

Owen Sheers
Feeling the Catch

It is four in the morning, and one lamp strobes me in its
                                                    stutter,
its filament fizzing, popping, fizzing
as water slugs by in the gutter.

I am here by the pub where things happened first;
the hot flush of whisky down the back of my neck,
the quick release in the alley out back.

There is a body shifting on the step of the doorway,
deep in its sleeping bag, a draft excluder caught the wrong
                                                    side;
a dirty blue chrysalis of dreams and cold.

But all I can think of is the heat in there,
the press of dancing bodies, the sheen of sweat,
piss steaming in a full ceramic sink,

three men round it, looking down, hands in front,
like picketing workers round a brazier,
or bowed head mourners at a funeral sermon.

And of Dai, doing his flaming Drambuies,
head back, eyes to the ceiling, mouth open wide,
singing hot notes of blue flickering flame.

How he used to make us lower the match,
that lit the pink, ribbed roof of his mouth,
before it caught and he felt the catch;

a flame from nowhere,
hot on his lips, which he would shut with a snap,
careful not to burn himself on his own blue breath.

And then his gasp, his long outward sigh,
and the shake of his head, like a horse,
bluebottles caught in its eye.

*

And now here, on this hill, where I came with you,
the girl in the red dress, whose name I can't remember,
on the only night we ever spoke.

Lying back on the bonnet of your father's car,
watching the house lights strike off,
shrinking the town to its tight centre.

Then looking up, constellations growing on the night sky;
following the curves of slow satellites
or the quicker release of meteorites: eighteen that night.

I never did see that dress, or you again.
Some told me it was because you were with Dai,
although I never knew and you never said,

but I still like to think I made an impression,
or at least left a reminder in the shallow dent
in the finish of your father's car –

right where it's hardest to beat out.

★

This was where Dai came too, eighteen that night
stopping above the valley's river of lights.

Unscrewing the cap like a bottle of squash,
and pouring it out over his thighs,

then lifting it, so it ran, thick over his head,
hair slicked down, an otter rising through water.

Then he must have lowered the match, careful,
waiting for the quick release and the catch,

which when it came set his body alive with fire,
flames quick at his finger tips, hot on his lips,

peeling at his skin, turning his hair to magnesium strips,
which fizz then pop then fizz.

And the car windows shatter,
shooting stars out,

glass constellations growing on the tarmac
with each pane's crack and burst,
while Dai, head back, mouth open wide,
burns himself on his own blue breath.

Nigel Jenkins
Some Lines to Request Poteen

Praise, Terry, your ace poteen
and praise be that Neath's heddlu
are averse, no doubt, to verse –
we want no drug squad readers.
These dry lines, cynghanedd free,
are sent to say I'm thirsty
for more of that cosmic juice
(spiritless bards are no use)
which, by the time I've finished
this, will have passed to the fish
of Swansea Bay, the bottle
ready to ferry this scrawl
across to Melincryddan's
spirit-maker number one.
Ice on fire, you're the poet
of where the contentions meet,
your wisdom's mirth an oak whorled
from the killing fields' antiworld
and your pained hands' outlaw love
for loves the world's afraid of.

It's late and getting later,
I'm a poet needs the fire
that only you can distil:
a Mumbler craves a refill.

Sláinte, then, and iechyd da
to Wales that voiced you, Eire
whose fatherly hand led you,
star by stream, to rebel muse
and old alchemical ways
with water, fire, fruit, barley.
Essence of unmachined rain,
most magical of moonshines,
clearer than ice and iced air,
though of suns the container;

exploder in the nostrils
of red orchards, dusty fields;
semen of the gods, hot blood
of goddesses, all falsehoods'
undressing when love defers
to the teachers and preachers;
song sprung from its silences
– bass of choirs, sky of pipes –
to set all atoms dancing,
the whole galaxy a-swing.
Each sip – and no 'head', thank god –
a fleadh cum wild eisteddfod.

The tide's in, the spirit's out:
be, Terry, on the look-out
for landfall on your doorstep
of this craft poteen-bereft,
barnacled and seaweed-draped
as proof of long, hard voyage,
weighed with verse and a bard's curse
on all hooch-busting peelers:
may every glass their thirsts crave
turn to boiling aftershave.
Here's a hope this plea finds you
stocked enough with cosmic brew
to save me from my drouth's hell
by filling full this vessel.
Hurl it then towards the stars
and I'll run from my boudoir
to catch it on re-entry,
Melin's gift to Mumbling me.
So pour, Ter, the nectar in
that's sure to set me writing
(light, awen, on this windbag!)
full cynghanedd – yn Gymraeg.
First and last I'll drink to you,
friend, bard and oaken guru.
Your spirit spells revival:
may your still be never still.

Stephen Knight
The End of the Pier

The pressure drops.
– Missing the sun
bay-fronted shops
on Bryn-y-Môr Rd
shut, one by one.
The day's forgotten
fruit goes rotten.
Yawns explode.

That stuff the sea
packs tightly in
a chest of sand
... perpetually
and anyhow ...
resurfaces now
as clouds begin
to cross the land.

– However slow
they are, days pass
and, every night,
looking for a ball
lost in long grass
thirty years ago,
the lighthouse light
finds nothing at all

along the coast
except for starfish
the waves discard –
giving up the ghost
until they're hard
enough to wish
upon – and then
the pier again.

My pockets are full
of pennies and sand.
A tugboat, I take
my daddy's hand.
I pull and I pull,
because he turns so
slowly in my wake,
and won't let go.

T.H. Jones
Brothel in Algiers: Wartime

Where the dark sisters paid
Their coins and charities
In landscapes of disgust
Waters and memories
Elusive, sad
Heretically recalled
Lust's younger season
And the ritual denied
The dance.

Here the humbling anonymity
Lost among the ascending spirals
The meagre ceremonies
Furtive observance
Wears and welcomes
Meek brutes and arrogant
And the world's wandering sons.

Ithyphallic demented choirs
Perform their unexultant rites
The sad priest blesses

Dance, o my daughters
For their short delight
Dance

These weary gyres are broken by small
                                    rooms
Where dirty beds invite
Where the sisters of charity display
Where the sons of violence are not afraid
Where is the deed
Walk nonchalantly up the crowded stairs
Through the smell of sweat
The smoke patterns and the stale, sour
                                    wine-breath
On the top floor they keep the rarities
Lean from the landing
And look down the gyres.

Who planted the great tree in the court?
Who plucks the tarnished fruit
From the insidious branches?

Sisters of mercy
I bring my prayer and the plucked fruit
To join you in the dance.

The priest dreams in the wilderness
The tall tree flowers
And the circles descend
And narrow
And the dance goes on

The sons of fear are violent
The sisters of display are charitable

Noise
And many smells
And coin changing hands

The deed
The dance
The darkness.

May 1948

Lyndon Davies
Journal d'un Fou

Light stretches out in an unbroken morning:
anything can happen now and it always does.
"Embalming fluid, jasper, myrrh and smaragd."
I'm rattling on downhill and the bike's a buzz;
or levelling out on the banks of the Seine.

Just killing time in the nest of massacres:
each bell a providence on a warbling square;
each lover poured from the spine. Secretions
gregariously disposed of. The bouquet of friends
at the gingham tablecloths in the bestial rooms.

It is only necessary to sit down
for this to begin again. There is no stopping
the magma, and no resort to ceremony:
Spring! In the suburbs opening to the skies,
I heard it beyond the wail of the asteroids.

White-Out

Everything I needed to say about the snow
eludes me now: every clause, each adjective,
frost-ravaged, chafed to the bone, is white
on white. The snow keeps coming and the bones
are buried deep as the celandine, as the lark's flight.

I couldn't see what I needed to see
on waking. A lustre broods on the gloom;
its thin, devotional glimmer pervades the room
and consecrates the ceiling. This is a light
which strands: the shame of the wardrobe turns from
   the shame of the tallboy.

Snow blocks the doors and divides the villages:
each separate wish in its separate reliquary.
I lie in wait for the dawn, for the smell of coffee
to open the cloaca, to spill its guts…
The rosary of the breath counts out its beads.

Hilary Llewellyn-Williams
Making Man

Something of stone, the heft of it
in your palm, the way it moulds
to the curve around your thumb –
the Venus mount – yet resists it:

something of wood, the rasp
of bark on your arm, the damp moss
smell, webs of xylem
packed sinewy in your grasp:

something of earth, the dense
and crumbled soil, dirt in the whorls
of your skin, muddy boots in the hall,
that clod indifference

out of which things grow
haphazardly, and jostle into form:
and something brutish too, the tossed horns,
rank sweat, stamped hoof, a bellow

in the frost, the way they stand
to piss, the hairy pelt and jaw,
and the old thrust and tumble;
the way they squint at the wind.

Inside, we're all the same:
thinking, and passionate,
bloody and soft, and fearful;
we all lie down to sleep, we all dream.

But outside it's the other, stark and raw
that makes the sap rise; the them
and us, the border, brother earth
and mother sea colliding on a shore

salt-tongued and dangerous.
So we said *let us make man*
from our own flesh and let him be
stone, wood, and beast for us.

Samantha Wynne-Rhydderch
Paramilitary Lover

He strokes my neck like the barrel of a rifle
he might have killed that German with,
his boots by the door, susceptible to the cold.
I glow by the fire in tandem with
the rosewood dresser, impartial to flames,
me with a passion for granite, him
with his head shaved against the night,
shedding his armour plate by plate.
I sleep under his shield, enfolded
in an English flag I think will
become my shroud. While I thrill
among the lilies, placing a chestnut
on the grate like a move in chess,
I see the incentive of lace
defeat artillery hands down.

Part of the Furniture

Since I had him stuffed
and mounted in a glass case,
my husband has truly become
what he always was:
part of the furniture.
Addicted to sitting still and staring
out of the window, now I've made sure
he can do that permanently.
I know he'd thank me for it.
Always wanted to be on display,
in his best waistcoat, the centre
of attention. Suits him: far better
disembowelled than drivelling on.

Lloyd Robson

three sections from Cardiff Cut

sunnyday but cold & slightwindy, gallopt inta town on the back of a cupa/bacon sarnie. turnd me ankle on corner of newport & fitzalan, leaping out the way of a taxi. nasty stitch in the bargain.

jumpt train wi no ticket as standard. rode the silverbrown doublescore to newport, graveltrack run of quadruple scars watchin steelbars curve soar curl across cities & moorland, via splottbridge hundred yards from me own front door, but no platform.

dock cranes & powerstat, transporter bridge & landfill site, westbound train goes passt window, inches from me glasssquasht nose in the corner of door well & toilet the corridor someone askt if i've change but i'm distant.

newport.

& no one on door / checkin tickets; from station to subway & the first thing to greet on this city street is the council tax / benefits office, black glassfronted bars, solicitors, estate agents.

hit of fresh rain & deplete of sun; the redburn of clouds stormwhipt from the door rush furnaces of llanwern; fumes from corridors of trucks ghosting the M4 coalscab delivery run / pavingslabs coming out of the sun / their cabs: mesht up; in convoy

the westgate hotel

john frost square:

gratis launch pissup: had me filla the grape, headed for a

rat&twat / pulld me escape, checkt out some bands (coupla wers down me neck) softrockers *ravensperm* & locally renowned *christstubble* & what a fuckin double act, covers of traditionals with their own inimitable superthrash theological throat cack, they get the crowd going mind. out.

drank up. considered parting the oceans but just one of the crowd taking part in the exodus up the street & city out. last thing i need is the gospel bouncing round on a fridee nite for fucksake or – *sweet jesu* – crying out loud.

waiting at newportstat: 2 boys use a third to batterram the chocy slot gob the lot chuck the wrap at each other's heads, skate off to the end; take a spliff stop to ease the bones chill cable drone of temper rods before they hiss & steam all over the platform.

headlow to take cardiff, catch the late again from paddington / the *devonport royal dockyard*, this territory chartered & homebound.
***
east cardiff:

(freightliner terminal: yellow travelling crane: bloke in the cabin: fag & the tellypage)

roath brook

rover way

white paint under splottbridge

> *'can't pay*
> *'won't pay'*

>> *'in emergency*
>> *press down the red handle'*

>>> inside the train.

★

reach mate's & buzz intercom; arrives late & reekina chips /
beer / sick & mildly blitzed, greasefingering me pockets for a
packet of skins & climbing the stairs without tumbling. inside
flat there is much chaos, perversion & despair; no expense
spared the margarine drips from floor to bread; the place is a
shithole but the food from the licensed premises downstairs
smells exquisite no less.

stick kettle on, build one, sit & stare, collect myself, take a
wash & while i'm there nick a fingerprint of toothpaste to get
rid of the taste from my taxi escapade. replace me hat&coat
& go give me mate an A. he takes it from silverfoil & downs
with his ale, puts down his glass & picks up a hammer from
the side of his chair & goes behind settee where i'm sat, pulls
out a brightly painted papier mâché fish which he places on
the table, sez

> *"right ya cunt; watch out"*

raises the hammer & pummels side of the
fish down to nothing dust. i didn't pick up on as quick as i
should / me feet propt on table flew from the wood little bits
of smithereen all over us

"fuck wha u doin!?"

but all is revealed: the belly fulla top quality marihuana flow-
erheads sown grown & flown over from south of the border
deep down mexico way

> *"our man in the americas; it arrived yesterday"*

we unwrap with care, both rewrap in 3skin with energy;
anticipate the first blast arome when we open the packaging,
the address label markt

> 'TNT".

(goodnite vienna, sut mae synchronicity...)

★

hit spar for late shopping; queue at the grill. bloke at the front asks

"*any milk?*"

assistant takes his key out the till walks along counter lifts flap negotiates half empty boxes spilt packs down the end of the aisle to the cooler cabinets at the back of the store (we entertain ourselves while he's gone), hallucinogens & stripglow of spar), picks up a pinta fullfat & returns to the counter, walks to the grill sticks key in the till hands over carton & sez

"*anything else sir?*"

bloke sez

"*i wanted skimmed*"

the queue goes uproar: half ina rush to get home; half off their faces & pissing themselves as assistant has ta go thro it allover.

we gess chatting to the girls ahead. they wait as someone serves us (we order beer / bogroll / loaf of bread, disposable lighters, chocolate / rizla / cigarettes, O & a coupla porkpies: buffet size, all they had). the staff say

"*enjoy yourselves/have fun/ be safe*"

knowing what they're selling & to whom & when (more than most of their customers *aware*; the girls on chocolate comedowns, the blokes grow impotent but too stoned to care).

girls in queue been drinking at angel hotel

angel hotel: where norman bates was arrested for possession

of cannabis posted from his missus in states; intercepted by customs & sent on its way; longhaul across atlantic for the sake of a setup fuh fucksake

the angel: where major major delivered a speech to the local representatives of the conservative party told them & the world how the city of cardiff was leading the united kingdom outa recession i mean: i still got an egg with his name on it

angel: where a student bumpt into a bloke off the box took her back to his overnite next thing his missus knows that missing paira boxershorts are front page headlines

the angel: jus down from the toucan & canton bridge where washup south walians who've jumpt in pisst at the prospect of never finding work / love / their home / their feet (the taff / ely / newport usk: none of em can cope with the rush; if the tides don't get em crohn's disease will shut the poor fuckers up); barmy balmy nites crossing canton bridge into riverside / überterritory across the city / self-proclaimed artists' quarter or *(fuckem)* muggers' paradise / sorry, not riverside, it's *pontcanna darhling*

the angel: over from the great shitbrain zoo where animals clamber walls / turn ta stone / attempt escape to the filthy orangefilter glow bouncing off shop panes over the walls of citycastle into backalley deaths & towercranes above the arms park...

spermspew gardens of sophia; prozzies, arseholes, mounted police on under cover coming to the sound of car alarms, hotwires, helicopters flashing over head, handcuff & baton fuelled by a desire to put this youngbastard to bed...

a reservoir of effluent breaks its dam / bursts taff embankments an orgasm uninterrupted by shitpushing dogs walkt by waterprooft wankers unaware of the parkbench shiftshank shafters of gaysex cardiff parks at nite, or maybe *aware*, that's why they go there: the loudest complaints from those who refuse to alter their route / cheap thrills for the righteous unaware it's their ilk who hide under moon & if unlucky: arrested: the zoo patrolled by titheaded horsefuckers riding beamfields / secret invasions litup & collared by legal uniform fetishists wank to a manjack of em; nocturnal promenaders kaarn av no privacy their individual wants trapt in public lavatories; getting what they want themselves then arresting their young devotees, satisfaction no guarantee of freedom. later released: the evidence didn't stick / still stuck in a copper's belly...

young cocks prod holes in chipboard panels / names & numbers scrawl promising examples of secret lust (who's most disgusting boys: those who write or us who damn? it's pretty fuckin obvious: *you doan wanna sucky suck*? then wait til st. mary street where real lads allowed the pavement as lavatory / where a canvas lion guards against cockwatchers / scatmongers / police officers as we chuck, piss & punch taxis / streetsleepers anything dulld enuf to hang long enuf ona bogstandard fridee nite down from the valleys, ready for the shuffling satdee shop crew who learn to shut their collective nose & mouth: most of em the very same lads can still make out their own little patch from the nite befor... someone burn the lion out before he sees tool anymore...)

the angel: the students in queue who invite us to party. a yeh. nice touch.

& the cheap beer claimed *premier* so we drank it while walking back down street & upstairs to settee, telly & music; prepare for the rest of the evening tho by now it's nite, clearly.

Owen Sheers
Night Bus

The girl with glitter in her hair
falls to sleep for a second against a stranger's shoulder,
leaves her mark; star-dust on his collar.

Two women with a mission get on,
placing themselves next to the lost, the forgotten,
slipping their pamphlet into half-curled hands.

She's falling again, her eyes flicking like a faulty screen,
dipping to darkness, sparking to light,
nodding her head in time to her own unconsciousness.

"Look to Jesus and he will save you,
he will show you the path to righteousness, the path to
                                             right.
Only he will show you the way."

And then her head drops, the inky hammer to the paper,
the judge's gavel, falling as slowly as only the guilty sees it fall;
but stranger, the young man in Wrangler, doesn't move.

Him and the driver, who counts them in, animals to
                                          the ark,
then shuts his doors, which hiss as they close,
a flat glass palm-off to the unsaved outside.

But then he moves his arm, a slow over-arm bowl,
over her resting head, then down across her shoulders,
a denim scarf of late night love, fingers stroking.

They're out of pamphlets, so the two women leave,
but others come to take their places,
sit and watch the scene behind their reflections, the
                                      day's credits roll.

Except for Wrangler man, whose own head has dipped now,
so he can smell the scent of her hair and kiss her there,
just lightly on the top of her head.

And isn't that what we all want anyway?
For love to come to us in our sleep,
to come to us here and now, when we least expect it?

She sinks deeper into her sleep, and deeper into him,
while his eyes watch the closed lids of hers,
and he tries not to disturb her with his breathing.

For love to get on and sit next to us,
to bring a halt to this night bus, and its endless midnight
                                                    ellipsis
of stops and stops and stops…

Graham Hartill
Silver John

"When evening shadows lengthen, it is not difficult to
believe that the reedy little tarn of Llyn Hilyn, near New
Radnor, is haunted by the spirit of a murdered man
whose body was thrown into it. The murdered man was
known as Silver John because of the silver button he
wore upon his coat. By some he is said to have been a
cattle drover, by others a skilful bone-setter and
charmer, especially expert in curing sick animals…"

1. A Dream Song of Silver John

I'll crack your joints stretched backward on a hay-bale,
then kick you good up the arse.
What's up?
            I'll yank your neck like a goose.
What ails you,
            that a kick in the balls wouldn't cure?

Crack your arm across your back
and haul you up like a bag of grass.
I'll double you up like a mouldy old carpet from out of some
old woman's kitchen.
I'll pull your spine so fast and straight you'll shoot all over the
straw.
You'll yelp like a cock taking fright at a fox,
it'll curdle the milk in the goat
and your back'll pull out straight and your knuckles go off
like a gun.
I'll kick your bladder around allover the barn,
and pummel your guts like a red-faced wife at the dough
board.
I'll claw them out and wrap them round your neck and pull
them tight till -
I'll tear your wick off and feed it to frisky hens.
I'll tug off your toenails and use them for fishhooks.
I'll rip out your glottis and stick it in mine and sing your
songs
then I'll go to your mucky house and and I'll murmur your
own sweet things to your daughter and wife and son.
Your tongue'll make a supper cheap for your fat blue cat.
I'll suck out your eyes then stick them back the wrong way
round,

so when I'm done you won't know whether you're coming or
gone –

*

2. Walking

Silver John is wandering the lanes from Kington to Builth.
He's covered himself with moons, which jingle between the
hedges. Money moons, his pay for broken ankles, black blood,
bedroom trouble. Owen pulled his shoulder out, heaving a
calf from a Welsh Black; Robson was born with a tangled leg,
a spastic branch, half-ripped from his hip. Now they're slav-
ing away in their barns again. John has been and gone.

He pummels the living daylights out of you, stretched dread-
fully over a bale. Now Silver John is treading his old familiar
line, humming his circuit. He takes his time today, it's sunny,
his collie scratches and twists on a yard of string. His hair is
matted brown, his jacket stitched from bits of a hundred
others. He smokes his scut and mutters his songs, the flutter-
ing of throatwings fills the familiar bending hill. He treads his
tunes on scabrous heel and toe.

He understands cows and dogs, and women, say one or two
women. At sunset, his jingling racket sets fire to polished
leaves along his way. Tomorrow a pint and a flake of silver to
toss you over a lump of hay and ring your ears. But now we
are walking along with John to the dark, later to be so secret
and bold and loud in the whispers and oily light of a high
valley cowshed.

*

3. His Sickness

Catch your own reflection in his buttons,
his 30x30 pieces.
Silver John's no saint,
  no healer,
  poet,
  priest.
Is not a man.

Silver John's mother put cakes all over your body,
  then chewed them, one by one,
her sin-eating song in her nose, full seemly.

He doesn't inhabit a house,
  or flat,
  or tent,
  or van.
He doesn't live nowhere.
John absorbs your illness.

You name it:
       gut-rot, mad cow, second childhood.
Viruses beg him to let them come to him.

He prays for them to infect his songs
   so that no-one can understand him.
He makes up stories about his granny's drum,
his Japanese sister,
   the moon he embraced.
His tongue is as hot as a horseradish.

No Jobseekers's Allowance,
SS snoops,
nor Neighbourhood Watch for John.
No Boots the Chemist or Marks & Sparks or Currys' frozen
                            doorways.
Just an ague, and a walk, a walk, a walk.

Don't fret,
he won't tell anyone about
   your itch,
   your dizziness,
   your vacancy.
You're safe with him.

This money he wears,
   is a thousand mirrors
and after all, your offerings.

★

Lay hairclips then,
and broken bits of mirror,
   corners of postcards,
   little plastic bulls,
   and smeared algae jam jars
down at his well, his watering hole.

Listen hard to the woodpecker,
learn his rattle.
And then to the tick of the wood beetle.

Welcome the moth to your thumb,
and the bat to your bedroom.

Stick your head in the fox's den
put Golden Syrup out for badgers.

Paint your breast with wasps.
Look after nature's people.

*

I'm hating and holding tight another wound-schism,
driving along in a whirl of domestic anger,
till finally a phone call finally puts the world to rights
and frees me to wander on,
to further dwell on those shiny coins
"that were his eyes", a coat
completely drenched
wherein his killers
saw themselves reflected,
protective mirrors.

The Radnor Boys pulled out his eyes,

So why did they ring the bells?
Getting shot of the scapegoat,
the Judas, showing off his (no, that's *our*) blood-money,
fear and jubilation,
guilt and liberation,
all drowned out in a golden, banging flood.

Scab-ridden kerb-crawler,
free-loading cunt of the ditches,
(might as well call them gutters),

who the hell did he think he is?
Well,
            he's just a story.

  Janice, an Irish woman, rings me up to talk about her stories:
"In the last few days you see I've lost my sight,
it happens from time to time since I had my stroke, well,
and I can't walk or write, so my carer Mary has to do it all.
I tell it all to her and she writes it down for me and types it
                                                    up."

  (In New Radnor church it occurs to me that the darkness
that smote the world when Christ died
was the horror of our not being looked upon.)
  "I'm sorry for ringing you up so early in the morning,
but I lose track of time you see."
I wonder did John fear "death by water?"
Driving tar-soft loops in some of the last and the few warm
                              days of the summer,
making do as my song-lines;
getting out, and walking round the churches,
eyes well peeled for ancient time-locks:
            Old Radnor – a foliate head (Victorian?);
the hillfort behind the church across the valley at New,
which stares straight back at the old coruscation 4 or 5 miles
                                          away,
where tucked away behind Old Radnor Hill, a shocking blue-
      white quarry lies silent in the Saturday warmth.

  I nearly twist my ankle circumnavigating the knobbly top of
                              the hillfort –
I should just be walking, not *writing* and walking
– such constant reminders of mindfulness come thick and
                              fast these days,
i.e., I nearly twist the *poem's* ankle.

These things are the metaphors,
            that is the *real* possibilities in poiesis.

While struggling over, (again, again and again) those different
                                                                    areas
                        of my psyche, call them "paths" perhaps,
wherein I'm still afraid or merely lazy, incapable of committing
                                            myself to one alone,
I hear my name called out, "Oh Graham"
Then later, wondering whether to buy his local cider, I realize
                                    that "Graham", in this case,
is a middle-aged, fat, asthmatic Spar keeper – and anyway, of
                                                                course,
it's just blurred vision – there is only one way – mine,
and "skilful means" do not preclude any good practice,
like doing everything in my power,
not to turn out like him, which is one ghastly possible reading
                                            of my karma.

This is the prize of my hunting today.

4. A Second Dream Song

Oak-roots heave at the gale-clouds
the sky is green and waving, full of fruit

Every babe is born with Deuteronomy on his buds
the sea is solid salt, as bare as brass

Every day a man goes fishing in his attic
helicopters flap about like gold-red fish in pools

Sailors, when they're hungry, far from home, eat fog
The King, that spider in a crown, craps oats

The sea pulls back, reveals the altar of the world –
inverted oak, its root-claws yanking at gales

*

Ending up at the 'reedy tarn', Llyn Hillin, where John was
                                            drowned,
to observe the molten, softly swaying, lemony green of the
                                            reeds
and the splash and the dip and the cruise of the coots.
Despite the cutting through of regular day-out traffic to
                                            Builth
and the barbed wire fence, it's beautiful,
shining blue in warm summer light, against the benevolent
                                    slopes of today's story.

The blue, the green, the fawn and the steel of the fence
and the red of the Citroen parked on the gravel,
resolve themselves to the white of the only outcome that
doesn't deny a thing.

                            *

      ... Some doggerel lines dating from about the time of the
      murder commemorate the crime, and in days gone by, it
      was asking for trouble to recite them within the hearing
      of a New Radnor man. The verse ran:

        Silver John is dead and gone
        So they came home a-singing;
        The Radnor boys pulled out his eyes,
        And set the bells a'ringing.
                      (Eric L. King)

5. Walking Towards His Death

Tonight my body's a tower of silence.
I'll die next Tuesday at half-past ten
not from cyanide or powdered granite
but tossed in a pond like a shit-tailed kitten
an insignificant village.

Out beyond the coast there was a country,
ancient roads lead nowhere to it.

A thousand died at Cantre'r Gwaelod,
the night Seithenyn, the floodgate guard,
got smashed on apple wine.
Now axe-welts shimmer in lapping water,
clumps of hawthorn, willow, fir,
and teacups drip from fishermen's hooks.

Out beyond the coast of what we know,
there's still a body,
places that recur.
Tuesday, I'll gulp down
pulverised diamonds,
and leap at the edge of your mind for good,
a slippery silver fish.

Pascale Petit
Seven Letters to My Mother from Dyffryn Lane

THERE ARE THE LETTERS I wrote when I was a child, that you kept for me to read after your death, and there are these letters that I have to write now, posting them into the earth of your grave – just enough room for my pages to grow into hundred-petalled books – hybrids the bees can pollinate. I write one letter for every day of this week, starting today which is Monday, the day I arrived at 7 Dyffryn Lane with my brother. I was seven, when I came to live with my grand-mother, and fourteen when I left, just starting my teenage. But you stopped all that.

Ma Mamie chérie,

We arrived in a heatwave, and no-one understood us. We whispered to each other in French and were hushed for being rude. I wrote letters telling you I did not want to go back to

Paris but I missed Toutou your poodle and wished you could bring him over. Long lists of those I loved included every animal I knew, and Papa, who visited once and took us to Chester zoo. Then I wrote letters that began in French and ended in English; letters in English with French spelling – "*slépeuse*" (slippers), "*réte*" (write). Our name for our strict new guardian – "Grammard" – stuck for many years. It was a nonsense word from our Franglais period, and I think we kept it because its sound evoked her power. But now I suspect there was a pun in it, the French "*grand-mere*" passing by way of our private 'grammar' into "*grand-merde*" – the pile of manure we'd been dumped in. For me she soon transformed like those cowpats that sprang into hares as I ran up to them but for my brother she remained the witch who boiled lights to feed her cats, whose starchy stew he spat out.

I struggled with the new language until great uncle Peter had the idea of a picture dictionary, and suddenly it was easy. I remember the words that were hardest to pronounce: the difference between "kick" and "cake". Kick was what my brother did to Grammard before she gave him the stick. Cake was what she baked when we were good. Soon, I was so good I was first in spelling at school. By the end of one year, I'd forgotten most of my French.

We arrived for the summer holidays, in a drought. A contract was signed that we were to stay for an indefinite period, that you were to send money and we would work in the house and garden. Although my brother says it was a workhouse, I do not think so. I loved the garden. I even loved the pump in the back kitchen where we used to take turns until all the tin tubs were filled, and the rare black roses saved. When I think of Grammard's house and its walk-in cupboards with their rags and broken knick-knacks, the back kitchen with the boiler, mangle and pump, the coalplace with the trunk of gipsy clothes for her to dress up to fortune-tell at fairs, hidden behind the coal, and the storeplace with its logs and cat-beds – I think of the special places on a man's body, places to hide and sulk, lying against the logs with all seven cats to stroke, my nose buried in fur.

I seal my first letter with 2027 kisses. Remember to look at the backs for the drawings!

Dear Maman,

Grammard's garden was a wide world. Her lawn was my savannah, her rockery my mountain, her shrubbery my jungle. Her rosebed a country I was only allowed to weed with supervision, treading lightly on the soft black earth that I draw and draw for you. Strawberries and cherries grew in the back garden. I didn't mind digging trenches for broad beans which I hate. I didn't mind sifting stones with the coarse and fine sieves, the stones that kept on surfacing like my memories of Paris – the grey courtyard cobbles of the school, the cellar where I had to count to a hundred before putting on the light, where I was glad for the door that kept the other kids out, once I had survived the dark and the fire-wolves at the bottom of the steps. The deeper I dug, the more stones emerged, as if an entire city was buried beneath the vegetables.

The harder I worked the more Grammard loved me. So I did not get beaten like my brother. Those times she caned me on the hands when you were there were only to pretend she was fair. And all because you'd found me 'sly' or 'deep'. Grammard said I was a willing worker, but the truth is I liked looking after her. I did not like looking after you, because however much I tried, you did not like me. I preferred helping Gwen Huws down the lane, with her orange make-up, husky voice, fancyman and six kids to make chips for. And old Mrs Jones nextdoor, who suffered from agoraphobia – I read to her then heated bread and milk in a saucepan on her bedroom fire. I preferred hand-feeding grass to the ewes with foot-and-mouth than cooking for you.

Dear Mummy,

I have three huts now – one in a hedge, one up the oak at the top of the lane (so I can spy on everyone entering it), and one under the roots of a tree in the woods above Berriew. The last one is the most important. It's where I keep my collection of 155 picture cards in an album wrapped in polythene. My favourite cards are: tropical animals, planes, wonders of the world, and birds. I also have some comical cards which I let my brother see, if we stop there when we run away. Today we ran away so far that we found the ruin where you used to live up in 'The Firs'. That's what Granny called it when we told her about it, after we'd given up and come home. It's just like you said! There are no doors inside and no glass in the small windows. The whole cottage would fit in our living-room! We sat on the roof and had our cherryade and fruit-cake, then we gathered wood as you used to, and placed it in the fireplace, in case we have to live there next time.

I'm glad we came back, because tomorrow there's a school trip to Lake Vyrnwy where there are 34 waterfalls! I'm taking my paints and book about bird facts so I can paint the birds for the school.

P.S. Notice the backs! The birds are a willow warbler and a yellow wagtail. I've also included two of my cards: trains and Interpol, and an opal fruit. They are for you to get better quickly.

Dear Mum,

It's Thursday already and I've so much to say before bed-time. Because I came home late I have to go to bed at six tonight. I waded across the river Severn, then went for a long walk on the far bank, further than ever before, so far that the tide was in when I had to cross back, so I had to swim. The current was very strong. Gran says my breasts are budding – that's what she calls it. I'm eleven and a half, more than halfway through my stay here, but I do not know this yet, that when they flower I will have to leave. Gran says I'm preco-cious because I'm French, but I still like to play with my dolls and china animals which sleep above my pillow. I'm back in my own room now. She said I wasn't to sleep with her any-more, putting my hands around her. She said it was dirty. I went to sleep for the last time last night with my hands carefully around her waist. She talked Urdu in her sleep again, and when I woke her she told me about the tiger that entered her tent in the Indian jungle when she was a baby. Now I know why she has a permanent tan.

I've started my periods. It happened when I was sitting on the outside toilet. I was trying like always not to look down at all the shit piled in the bucket of Jeyes Fluid under the wooden seat, holding my breath because of the smell, and keeping an eye on the spider in the corner. There was blood on the paper and I was scared something was wrong. Then Gran told me what it was. I had a feeling in my tummy like when I'm swimming across the river and the tide's in. The current pulls me under the tree roots on the far bank where there's a tramp's mattress near the rat-holes, my foot scratched by the rusty car in the whirlpool.

Dear Maman,

I'm sorry I called you Mum. It's what the other kids call their mothers here, it isn't a deodorant. I must tell you about the floods, how the fields turned into seas. We set out, O.P. and I (that's what I call him now), to fetch cracked eggs from the farm down the lane, and after we passed the dolmen, the lane vanished where it dips. We could see two horses marooned in a high corner of the field, and a sheepdog swimming about trying to get the animals in. A man was stranded on top of his car in the layby. The helicopter that rescued him passed over us – we were on the news!

Gran lets me go to bed at a quarter to seven now, but O.P. still has to go at six because he's naughty. I didn't like it when you told me she used to fix the clocks, that we went up the dances at five. Time has its floods and droughts, and just as there were extra hours in clocks, so I found extra stories in books. There were only five books in her house (apart from the gardening ones), and during those long light summer evenings when we used to hear the Huws children playing in the back field, I reread the books. I'd stop halfway through a paragraph and concentrate until a new story appeared that felt so real, it would be there next time I passed that chapter. In this way, the woman in the Western had a fancy-man and only I knew when they met. And God said different things to Abraham in the cartoon bubble. While other stories disappeared. It was like not being able to get through the lane. I'd skim across a few words swimming about, see Billy the bull chained to a tree on the riverbank by the ring in his nose, slowly sinking into the mud. There were stories that leapt from fields like lambs in Spring, their wet noses nuzzling my hand, stories hot and bristly as the backs of pigs. I made them real and time flew.

I wrote birthday books for my brother, so time would fly for him too. I sewed pages together until they were thick as an igloo he could snuggle into, surrounded by my stories, drawings, rhymes and puzzles. I made books that he could give back to me on my birthday, that I would read as if I had never written them. I wanted the sun and the snow and the rain to have written them.

Dear Maman,

Last night I went on my first date, with Glyn the farmer's son from the Evans farm at the bottom of the lane. Gran made me stand on the table to see if my skirt was too short. I must think carefully about what happened, how she must have seen us kissing in his car at the gate, because today she looks white writing her letter to you. After all the letters she wrote begging you to take us back (which I've read now), she's throwing us out. But he kissed me so fast I didn't have time to think she could see. Afterwards he unbuttoned his shirt and I leant against his chest. I felt like I was trampling a path through a ripe cornfield – the expanse of it, the blond hairs, the smell of the seeds in their husks, the risk that the farmer might shoot me for trespassing. I thought how I could live my life there, listening to the bees crawling out of poppies, their thighs packed with pollen.

But you put an end to mascara and pink lipstick and my red miniskirt and white fur jacket with the leopard spots. You said they were cheap. I had to forget Gran's slutty ways, fold my school uniform neatly, and have my long hair cut, and forget about boys.

Sorry this is a short letter, but Gran says we must hurry and catch the post before she changes her mind.

Dear Mother,

Today is the last day. My end-of-year report says I'm too quiet, but can't you hear me shouting inside this page? I have the runs, but Rex is locked in the toilet because he won't stop barking, even though he's been dead two years, so I can't go. O.P. is quiet for once. What we need to know, what we're asking, in whispers that crack the glass on Gran's treasure-cupboard is: can the animals come with us? Gran won't answer. Ernie, Elvis and all the cats are curled in their silences. Even Adam the budgie for the first time in seven years is quiet.

When we leave I will never think about any of them ever again.

Now we are stationed at my bedroom window, watching for your taxi to wind its way down from Welshpool. We can smell your perfume already, as we always could, before you arrived for the holidays.

We've been for a walk down the lane, tried to look at everything properly, as if we weren't bored by the old swing tree and wasp tree, the sheep that look so friendly until you stare into their eyes. Every cow has a black and white map painted on her sides – black for lies and white for truth, or whitewash, for you to talk deep into the nights to come, washing away all trace of Gran. We've said goodbye to the Tanners and their ferrets, to Gwen Huws who in one year will fall downstairs during a fit and choke on her vomit. To Mr Jones who one year later will hang himself from our favourite climbing tree. To Dai Jones his son, Gwen's fancy-man, who used to shadow us on our riverside walks, who sat me on his knees once and slipped his fingers inside my knickers, so that Gran had to ask if I'd enjoyed it. I won't know what she meant for years now. I haven't packed my miniskirt, my rabbit-wool jumper, nor the black lace suspender-belt that shocked you so. We've said goodbye to the dolmen and Ned the postman's ghost.

I'm posting this last letter into the earth, at the end of a neat row of letters furled like bulbs. I expect a blaze of flowers, with petals like the pages of books no-one has read yet, in any language, written by the dirt and its browns and blacks, and all its stones, which are the clouds of your sky, as you lie looking up.

P.S. Don't forget to look at the backs! Don't forget that every word has a picture on its back, that the more you made me disappear inside my words, the bigger the pictures grew.

Landeg White

As Goldfinches are Stabbing the First Green Cones

There are plants, for example, so whole-hearted
in their being, you don't need to wait
for their fruits to attest them.

Lemon trees are lemony to the tips of their newest
mahogany buds, no mistaking a lemon for a mere grapefruit,
or toning its acids down with horse manure,

and basil, just walk past it, and the whirl of air's
enough to permeate the whole walk way.
Or eucalyptus, best after a shower,

with its silver-fish foliage and striped-plasticine bark,
the merest sun-dried sliver of which
radiates its camphor. Alice broils

pumpkin leaves with the yellow flowers and a speckled
pumpkin egg, the milky chlorophyll pulsing throughout.
Or take pine trees this July evening as

goldfinches are stabbing the first green cones, just
scratch the trunk, and the weeping's pure pine.
Then there's walnut trees with their dedication

to silverplate bark and silver green foliage
and their incorruptible nose-cone hardness.
As for vines, already their leaves are predicting

October's purple and white musts. It's how I
was taught, and I still reckon, a poem should be
to the least comma

(though, of course, there's also much to be said for lying).

Sarah Corbett
Green Rose

First, I was tenderly young.
Second, I believed myself empty of sex.
So when I sickened, ballooned,
I thought it was fear breaking
out of its egg at last.

Your father kicked down the door,
dragged me by the hair
and raped me in the cold backyard.
How was I to know of your heat
in that bitter pod inside?

When, at twelve weeks, I heard
of your presence, your Thumbelina
arms, legs, spine perfecting
in the walnut shell of my womb,
the black earth bloomed.

OK, I engineered your death,
but woke after wanting you back,
searched all the rubbish bins
in all the backyards from here to Liverpool,
broke my teeth at the clinic walls.

You are my daughter of the green rose,
you demand water daily. You root,
put out leaves to catch my rain.
Your closed buds never flower
but hold tight the colour of my crime.

Stephen Knight
The Loved Ones

Perhaps we played outside
all afternoon, climbing the slide
while they stole away
... it must be years and years ago;
and, busy growing up,
we were slow to ask our parents
exactly when they left for ever.

– What happened then?
Perhaps they haunted
Ravenhill Park for days on end
then shuffled home to lie
awake all night, knitting
unwanted socks.
If brooches, clocks, linen

or best china reach us
years later we remember
all their fussing
when we were three years old.
Those thin hands we held
(Forgive us) so reluctantly.
Their crumpled skin.

Or else we apologise,
smile even,
because we can't begin to testify
how wise they were, how fierce;
because we can't recall
the colour of their eyes.

We had an orange ball:
we used to laugh:
we used to sing and shout:
and if we thought at all
we had no doubt.

Perhaps we played outside.
Perhaps the sun was out.

Carol Rumens
The Quest, the Hex, the Alkahest

Hate – what a whirlwind ride
From love to there:

Star into black hole, white-hot Mr Hyde
Into flaky Jekyll –

Believe me, this
Wasn't like turning a coin.

It was radical re-design.
So I gathered glass blackberries

From the only rose too wise
To wear fancy suits

– The *Alchemila vulgaris*
And revised my solvents and solutes.

I'd been chucked out of O Level
Chemistry (Cookery, too)

But I knew how to blacken a name,
Cure desire and divine the healing kiss

Sent in a bubonic bubble
Of spit: if love was shit, whatever else

Would be no syllogistical trouble.
I turned up the flame, threw in

A flash of salt: as soon as my world of dew
Rose to the boil,

I added the can of worms, the tin of stew:
The love-thing. Oh, it glowed

Deeper the longer it rode,
Slow-tanning to a hepatitis shade

In an ooze of gas on the hollow
Crux of each second-hand ring

I rented as I travelled.
I knew I was chemical king of the rolling
                                                    road

When water was just a ghost
On a distant cheekbone (whose

I didn't care – not mine
Any more, ever, amen)

And I stroked its face as the matter cooled
And I called it *the most*

Malleable and ductile
Metal, miraculous *gulth,*

Glitter of wealth in the froth
Of my gullible self

– No, wait. I was better than that.
I called it hate.

I'd lost my sense of shame.
Soft parts are first to get fucked

As that Hazchem Eucharist
Rinses your mind, but

It's the bargain you strike
For the twenty-two carat product.

I played with the target, zapped
Some shy peripheral *putti*

(Split-splat) then aimed point-blank
At the former seraph

– You. I wanted blood and tears, no pity,
So here was the set-up:

Your favourites walked the plank
In front of you. I had you widowed, jailed,

Tortured, on fire, hanging from a spike,
Gnawed out by cancers,

Wild-eyed with Alzheimer's,
Laid low by machete attack.

Blood? It was only ketchup,
The *kitsch* of the poor, the *kvetch* of the
                                    hated,

Bouncing back, twisting the tale
Begun with your very own knife

Thrust through my hero's life: reversal,
Darling, the oldest trick:

Revenge, if you like. Now, though,
It had your sheen, your brow:

It would last forever, my septic
Passion, tender and true

As erectile tissue,
Secreting radiant ink

Like the real thing. Not so.
Think, if you dare,

How the dead live. A new
Corpse is a gas,

All go in its green-blue-pink
Bio-bright kit, it dances

A day or two, yes,
Then slithers off back to bed, lies down

Abandoned, random, done.
When the last degradable bit

Has gone, the glamour has.
And hate's like that.

Dead love is jazz. Dead hate is zilch,
Zero, the emptiest flat

In the writer's block, the binned obit.
It's a legless bug, a glugless sink:

It's darkness visible
– But you need to be Milton to see it.

After a final belch
At the dizzy alchemist

To deliver (*cover and duck!*) a knock-out hit
Of isopropyl methyl-

Phosphorofluoridate,
It pisses off to wherever

Stork lies down with butter.
And maybe, somewhere, the difference
                              doesn't matter:

Base and Precious wed in a silvery mist
On an aisle in some Tescos

For stars – that's Chemistry
For girls. But Alchemy? Sheer spin

And greed, like the other thing
Which makes the world go round

The twist and reappear
Decidedly pear-shaped.

Don't think I'm being moral:
Given a local fount

Of elixir, a pinch of salt,
A body that seemed to count,

I'd kill tomorrow.
But no-one's there. Or here.

Hyde snuggled back inside
Jekyll (*Look, no hair*).

Dew's dew. My rose, you
Aren't much of a rose

Since the alkahest jumped cup.
Tin, of course, continues

To be tin: functional, cold,
Often found empty. Gold? We made it up.

Paul Henry

Acts

There are months of not loving you
when the plates we keep spinning
simply spin – but today I woke
and broken china surrounded the bed.
Today was loving you again.

I limped into a small garden,
knowing that soon, in spite of us,
the plots of soaps would drone on,
the commentaries from transistors
on allotments, the bees in the fuchsias,
the trains slowing down or gathering speed
with somebody on them thanking Christ
they don't live here, or there ...

I have given up trying to piece together
so many broken plates, to perfect
the circus acts of love.

                        I remember
that once, in the sun's spotlight,
our dust made a merry-go-round.
I remember a rippling field
and sand slipping from under our feet.

I remember that much of loving you.

                    ★

One shirt, one dress on a line
(such acrobatics – the leaves hold their breath
and then applaud) yours and mine –
the closest we'll come to a fall.

                    ★

How is the knife thrower?
Of all the eyes in the audience
he picked out yours. And so it was that,
after he'd made you his squaw,
I watched you turn weak at the knees

and somewhere, beneath all the smiles,
heard the lions roar.

                    ★

There are months of not loving you
when the lion tamer's charm is enough.
She's easily as brown as you
and the jungle in her eyes
matches the ocean in yours.

But when she leaves the cage ajar
an impulse makes for your shore.
                    ★
Today the strongman cracked.
The tributaries in his neck
erupted with lava.
His fixed grin crumbled
and an avalanche of teeth
bit the dust.

When he fell
the whole house shook and the weights
spun off the end of all he'd held dear.

Glancing in the mirror he saw
Saturn without its rings,
Christ without his halo,
the Mona Lisa without her smile,
a universe of ash ...

★

There are months of not loving you,
empty domes for the mildly insane,
where The Prozac Clowns rehearse. ..
'Timing, timing is everything!'
calls Zac to Coco (on his arse
with a blade through his brain).

And there are days, tumbling days
that blur your face,
when the woman spinning by her smile
could be anyone.

But not this day.
I missed you in the lunch-hour crowd,
the pull and push of its currents
beneath my aching feet

and every so often,
through tears in the canopy,
your blue eyes staring back
from another time.

Pascale Petit
My Mother's Mirror

Your make-up mirror
has a milky blue cast over it
like the eye of a snake
preparing to moult.
I am standing naked in your room
and you're painting me blue.
I don't know how I got here
or why your face shimmers
like a mirage through the Gitane haze
as you fasten copper bells around my neck,
teeth bracelets around my wrists.
You lead me to your dressing-table
which is two steps away
but seems far off as Chichén Itzá.
When you push my face into something cold –
I know it's just a small round make-up mirror,
not the Well of Sacrifice.
But when you tip it magnifying-side up –
jaws unlock
like a snake swallowing our house.
Into your mirror I fall,
down the long body of the Well,
past limestone shelves
ridged like a serpent's spine,
right into the rattler,
the tail-cone at the bottom,
the silver sludge of the glass,
where I lie
for what feels like a thousand years.

I surface in the glare of a Mayan forest.
Archaeologists pull me
out of the stinking waters.
They reconstruct my last day
from fragments of painted ceramic jars,

bracelets of teeth,
copper death-bells
and a carved stag-antler
I might have bought in the market
before I came home to find the god waiting.
They say I was proud
to be chosen by the plumed serpent.
I arched my back over the rock
and let the priest knock out my teeth
for the next child's costume.
Through the red mist
that flowed from my mouth over my eyes,
I must have blinked twice
after the gold-plated knife
was plunged in my chest.
I must have seen my heart
raised up to the sky.

Zoë Skoulding
Your Kidney Sings

I.

Your kidney sings to mine
through skin and air. Our livers leap
like dark fish swimming home
through wine-red floods; four lungs
nestle together, black wings rising
and falling to the same beat of blood.
The three-year graft survival rate
for spouse-to-spouse living
donor transplants is 85%.

2.

Issei Sagawa - how she rolls
his name around her mouth,
celebrity cannibal-to-be
(after the gunshot and her silence).
Now he's getting right
under her skin, her body open,
every juncture losing meaning,
tissue torn apart, fissures
in the flesh, this puzzling silence –
and all he wanted was
the light that came from her.

3.

There's rain outside, a wind
that sends everybody mad;
I'm drenched in seconds, water
streaming down my neck,
delirious on the doorstep,
fumbling with the key

while out at sea the waves
crash shattered phrases on the rocks:
I it you love don't we;
consume the land which crumbles
at their touch; it was only sand
and now it's shifted into masses under sea.
Foreign matter sluices in, the alien
salts and fishscales, broken glass
which once held liquids we wouldn't
know the names of, intoxicating
tides which wash away
the sand, the soil, which lighten us.

Patrick McGuinness
Days in the New Country

Newborn beings emerge from the Arrivals
lounge, sniffer dogs and luggage snapping
at their ankles. Behind plate glass walls, streets

sway in the heat, breathe like faraway furnaces.
Passports stamped, beyond the sliding door
visa, vista: both lay the country at your feet.

*

Along broad avenues the trees
are on patrol, portraits of the Leader
like lopped heads cradled in their branches.

Loudspeakers murmur slogans for the ear
to slide off. In the spaces between trees,
guard dogs doze beside spectacular militia.

*

The year peters out into a tail of power failures,
food shortages, a detritus of old calendars,
unfindable spare parts for broken Chinese toys.

Always a street away, Orthodox chant;
incense tracing prayer's trajectory, making prayer
visible, as dust brings out an arc of light.

*

Then the season of frozen fountains;
the Boulevard of Socialist Victory
in perpetual mid-construction.

Gypsies beg, are beaten and moved on;
no-one cares, they don't exist: optical illusions,
revenants, the sleeve-tugging of gone days.

*

The waitress in the pirated *Coke* T-shirt
that reads *You Can't Stand the Feeling*
recites the menu like a roll call of extinct species.

241

In the Natural History Museum,
the extinct species are making room.
Birds are silent by the treeful.

            ★

Events hold their breath, as if unsure whom
to happen to. Then they're overtaken by events:

the Ceausescus standing on their balcony
as the cheering turns to jeering. To them
both looked the same; too high to tell
how power spares the powerful the very
understanding that might spare them.

            ★

A week takes place in spurts, as on a newsreel.

Footage of the ransacked ministries,
broken statues, the teargas that unleashed
the tears that bubbled up through cobbles,
feathered up from drains and hydrants,
from the cracked tarmac of the motorways
to the crazy paving of the presidential palace.

Underneath the flagstones is the beach.

            ★

The trial is filmed inside a bunker:
he puts out a grainy hand to guide her

through the darkness. Later, slumped
against the wall, their faces are composed;

the backs of their heads lie beside
them like a dropped disguise.

The revolution is a slipped mask.
They are free to be themselves at last.

Rhian Saadat

Souvenirs from the Voyages of d'Urville and Dumoulin

Apart from the head-dress with the white and black feathers,
there will be an atlas with fifty-two, never-before-seen maps
of another side of the planet. And there will be a dugout's
                                                    prow
from the Solomon Isles – a head with wide-open eyes,
                                                guarding
sailors against the sea's bad spirits.

La terre promise, the explorers called it, coming home,
                                            emptying
Astrolabe and *Zelee* of their treasures – pumice stone people
from the Admiralty Isles, fish hooks from the Society Isles,
                                                    spears,
axes, ethnic bones and a club from the Marquesas' *u'u* tribe,
with a remarkable patina of wear and tear and passing time

and a collection of many curious dolls, from the Hopi and the
                                                    Zuni
of New Mexico – each one carved from a single root of the
                                                aspen tree
and painted colours accorded to the Compass points – black
                                            for the zenith,
the nadir of it – grey, with a final addition of amulets and –
                                        again – feathers,
giving Dumoulin's bulging corvettes an aspect of their own
                                                plumage

as they settle themselves upon the cool, familiar rim of their
                                        world. The dolls
will later be prized by exiles, charmed by their childlike
                                patterns – consumed
by their unfaded expressions of startled loss.

Paul Groves
Man and Boy

My father used to get a six-inch nail,
position it above the little 'eye',
and give one hammer stroke. If all went well
he would not need another to gain entry
to the hidden heart. Maraca-like,

it had been shaken roughly near an ear.
Once I had heard that distant inner lake
it became time to taste its magic water.
The coconut smacked of an old ape's breast,
fibrous and alien. Spike extracted,

my father raised the fruit as if a blest
offering, and carefully enacted
the ancient ritual. I sampled next.
We changed to sucklings at a sacred pap.
No word was said. This went below all text

into a tribal memory. The sap
was drained, and then the butchery began.
The wooden ball was placed on a flat stone
and axed into two halves. He lifted one
and left the second portion, which was mine.

Meic Stephens
Extract from 'Poetry Wales at 40'

LET ME GIVE YOU some idea of the Wales with which I
had to get to grips shortly after coming down from
University in the summer of 1962, when I was twenty-four.
My first job was teaching French in Ebbw Vale, still a steel-
making town in those days, and I was living, with Harri Webb

and others, in Garth Newydd, a large, ramshackle house in Merthyr Tydfil that no one seemed to own. Harri, an old Republican and by then branch librarian in Dowlais, was doing a stint as editor of *Welsh Nation*, Plaid Cymru's news-paper, and I used to lend him a hand, thus learning the rudiments of editing, typefaces, layout and proof-reading: a useful apprenticeship as it turned out. We were both active in the ranks of Plaid Cymru – I stood, quixotically, against the veteran S.O. Davies as the party's candidate at the General Election of March 1966 – and, because we had only squat-ters' rights in Garth Newydd, we felt obliged to keep the door on the latch for assorted Nationalists and Socialists, and a few fellow-travellers, from other parts of Wales.

Our immediate concern, as left-wingers, was to challenge the dead hand of the Labour Party in 'the rotten borough'. But we also made excursions further afield, particularly when *Cymdeithas yr Iaith Gymraeg* began raising the stakes by holding demonstrations in favour of official status for the Welsh language in campaigns that often resulted in fines and imprisonment. I was among a gallant band who, in February 1963, took part in the society's first demo: we sat down on the road at Trefechan Bridge in Aberystwyth, holding up the traffic for an hour or so in an attempt to get the town's mag-istrates to issue summonses in Welsh. With John Davies, the society's secretary, I drove around Wales coaxing sub-post-offices to put up bilingual signs and removing road-signs that offended us because they were in English only. The Welsh language was the engine driving youth revolt in this part of the world and, although I didn't speak it as fluently as I do now, I was happy to put my shoulder to the wheel.

What had brought Harri and me, along with a few thou-sand others, into the Nationalist movement was the drowning of Cwm Tryweryn to make a reservoir for Liverpool against the wishes of the people of Wales and their elected represen-tatives, and we were usually to be found among those who, in defiance of the party line, favoured what was euphemistically called 'direct action'. The saboteurs David Pritchard and David Walters, 'the Boys from Gwent' as a popular ballad called them, were regularly under our roof, and Emyr Llewelyn (Jones), who was imprisoned for his part in damaging an electricity transformer on the site of the dam, was an occasional visitor. More generally, we called for the creation of a Welsh Office and a Secretary of State for Wales as first steps in a process of devolution of power from London to Cardiff which has still not produced the Parliament we wanted; we heckled at Labour meetings and were wary of anything introduced by the Tories; we drew attention to the case for allowing Plaid Cymru to make party political broadcasts by painting slogans on walls and speaking on the clandestine Radio Free Wales; we welcomed any sign of cultural renewal and fresh, radical thinking about the arts in Wales; and we mocked the humbug of Labour politicians like Jim Griffiths and the Uncle Tom attitudes of the picayune George Thomas to the question of self-government and the Welsh language.

As Harri wrote in his squib 'Merlin's Prophecy 1969': 'One day, when Wales is free and prosperous / And dull, they'll all be wishing they were us.'

There was, too, an awareness of the wider world. We protested against the war in Vietnam, the proliferation of nuclear weapons, the apartheid regime in South Africa and the British presence in the six counties of Northern Ireland. We argued macaronically about Frantz Fanon's *Les Damnés de la Terre*, Raymond Williams's *Culture and Society* and Richard Hoggart's *The Uses of Literacy*.

Then came Gwynfor Evans's victory at the Carmarthen by-election of July 1966, followed by very high polls for Plaid Cymru in Rhondda and Caerffili. Harri and I both believed, moreover, that politics and poetry weren't mutually exclusive and could, as in France and Spain and Russia, for instance, be complementary.

I still think that not to have been affected by the political events and social conditions of the early 'sixties, in Wales and the world, and not to have written about them, would have been tantamount to gross irresponsibility and mere aestheticism on the part of Welsh writers. I had been involved in various literary and political activities at Aberystwyth, where I'd edited *The Dragon*; and during my year in Bangor, where I'd talked about a new magazine over innumerable cups of coffee with Tony Conran, but it wasn't until 1962, in the heady ambiance of Garth Newydd, that I began to do something about it.

In this I was helped not only by Harri but by Keidrych Rhys, the former editor of *Wales*, who used to visit us from time to time, although some of his gnomic advice went clean over my head: "Never trust a writer who wears suede shoes, dear boy, or a Welshman who signs himself 'Yours ever'". Be that as it may, the first thing I did during the harsh winter of 1962/63, when we were snowbound in Garth Newydd, was set up the Triskel Press, an imprint on which I published *Triad*, a selection of thirty-three poems by Harri, Peter M. Griffith (later Gruffydd) and myself, with a preface by Tony Conran, which served as a kind of declaration of intent. Among those who welcomed our booklet in the Welsh-language press were Aneirin Talfan Davies, Jac L. Williams and Gerald Morgan; the English-language media in Wales virtually ignored us. By the time the thaw was under way a few weeks later our booklet had sold 500 copies and so it then seemed a logical step to start a literary magazine.

Whatever my aims may have been, I knew the field to be a stony and marshy one. Apart from the *Western Mail*, which in those days had a literary page carrying poems, stories, articles and book-reviews, the only journal dealing with the literature of Wales in English was *The Anglo-Welsh Review*, edited in England by Roland Mathias. With the arrogance of youth (a touch of which isn't all that bad a thing, I can't help feeling) I threw a few barbs in his direction because the *AWR* seemed to me a bit out of touch with the reality of life in Wales. There was also *The London Welshman*, a monthly edited by the genial Tudor David, a professional journalist; the first issue of the cyclostyled *Second Aeon*, edited by Peter Finch, was a year off. Harri and I enjoyed working with London-based writers like Bryn Griffiths, Sally Roberts (later Jones), Tom Earley and John Tripp, who had come together to form the Guild of Welsh Writers, which was to help prepare the ground for the creation in 1968 of an English-language section of Yr Academi Gymreig.

But as for Welsh writers in English, there weren't very many. All the ones I knew, at least by reputation if not personally, appeared in the inaugural number of *PW* in April 1965. They included (besides myself) Harri, Peter, Roland, Bryn, Alison Bielski, Robert Morgan, Douglas Phillips, A.G. Prys-Jones, Alun Rees, John Stuart Williams and Herbert (Lloyd) Williams; the English poet Robert Nye, then living in Montgomeryshire, the expatriate David Elias and Ida M. Mills made up the first fifteen.

There was neither editorial nor review in the first number's eighteen pages but Gwyn Jones, my old English Professor at Aberystwyth, wrote a short memoir of T.H. Jones, the poet who had recently drowned in Australia. I like to think Gwyn's contribution suggested a sort of continuity with his *Welsh Review*, which had put up the shutters as long ago as 1948. I was quickened, too, even as I corrected the galleys, by his note in the London Welsh Association's St. David's Day programme: "That there is no new or better *Wales* or *Welsh Review* appearing in Wales today is inexcusable. That there is no little magazine which would allow us to see and sift the poets is shocking. The best thing that could happen to Anglo-Welsh letters just now would be the emergence of some piercingly bright and original talent. The second best thing would be the appearance of an exciting but authoritative journal which would give young creative writers their chance but not cosset them. The first of these desiderata would be an Act of God; but the second is quickly compassable by any man worth his salt. The difficulties are many, and the problems complex – but then they always were. In a rough and ready way writers get the journals they deserve. Is there no Welshman now breathing who can provide one?" Thus was the gauntlet thrown down and, my resolve stiffened, I picked it up.

As many a simple patriot has found to his cost, it's easy enough to bring out the first issue of a magazine: the hard bit is distributing and selling it, and then bringing out the second and third. I printed 500 copies of the first number of *PW*, paid the printer £47 4s (a fortnight's salary in those days) and six guineas for a cover design by Aubrey Jones (an art student known to us as Aub the Daub), and decided to sell it at three shillings a copy. This cover price left only a slim margin and, had the magazine been sold mainly at a discount in the shops, I would barely have recouped my production and distribution costs. I therefore decided to sell the magazine direct to readers. In this I relied mainly on friends, within and without Plaid Cymru, and on a handful of people willing to act as my agents in other parts of Wales and in London. A month later we had sold out. The same thing happened with the second and third numbers (except the printer's bill went up to £85 2s for 48 pages), so that by the Winter of 1966/67, by which time I had more than a hundred subscribers and sales were still holding up, I was able to bring out pamphlets in the Triskel Poets series by Herbert Williams, John Tripp and Leslie Norris (now collector's items), with cover designs by David Tinker, as well as 3,000 copies (print cost £479) of a substantial paperback by Gerald Morgan, *The Dragon's Tongue*, about the fortunes of the Welsh language.

The only subsidy from public sources received by the Triskel Press during its first two years was the sum of £40 for five numbers of *PW* from the Welsh Committee of the Arts Council (as it then was), which was less than a tenth of our print bill and barely enough to pay for envelopes and stamps, though it was a start. The administrative chores, of which there were a great deal since accounts had to be kept and correspondence and invoices neatly filed, was carried out by my wife Ruth, whom I married in August 1965. She it was who also ensured a croeso for the hungry poets who began calling at our house in Twynrotyn and later Rhiwbina, after our move to Cardiff in the summer of 1966, when I became a reporter with the *Western Mail*. It wasn't until 1968, my having been appointed Literature Director of the Welsh Arts Council (as it would soon become), that *PW*, together with all the other literary magazines of Wales in both languages, began to receive subsidy.

Soon it seemed that Welsh poets writing in English were springing up as if the field had been sown with dragons' teeth. I recently counted the names of those who contributed to the magazine's first seven numbers, that is up to Winter 1967 (vol.3, no.2), by which time I had handed the editorial reins, *dros dro* as it turned out, to Gerald Morgan and Gwilym Rees Hughes. They were 56 in all. Some, like Harri Webb, Bryn Griffiths, Alison Bielski, John Stuart Williams, Peter Gruffydd, Raymond Garlick, Alun Rees, Tony Conran and John Tripp, contributed to almost every number, and they were joined on a regular basis by Roland Mathias, Robert Morgan, Leslie Norris, Dannie Abse, Emyr Humphreys, Sally Roberts Jones, Joseph P. Clancy, John Ormond and R.S. Thomas; with the exception of Joe Clancy, all these were also represented in 'The Lilting House', the Dent anthology I co-edited with John Stuart Williams in 1969. Among the Welsh-language poets who sent at least one poem to what our title-page proclaimed as "Cylchgrawn Cenedlaethol o Farddoniaeth Newydd" (I'm glad this rubric has survived the years) were Euros Bowen, Gwyn Thomas, Derec Llwyd Morgan, Gwilym Rees Hughes, Pennar Davies and Gilbert Ruddock.

I see from the entry in *The New Companion to the Literature of Wales* (UWP, 1998) that 'Under the editorship of Meic Stephens, who took Irish and French magazines as his models, *PW* was national in outlook, but not narrowly so. Among its concerns was the fostering of mutual interest between writers in the two languages of Wales'. True, I had certain Irish and French magazines in mind, particularly John Jordan's *Poetry Ireland*, which he'd revived in 1962, but also some of the more combative magazines put out by Hugh MacDiarmid, whose example in trying 'to break the living tomb' of Scottish letters I hoped to emulate.

I've said enough about the Zeitgeist of Wales in the 1960s to suggest why I had to make *PW* a national magazine. I wanted it to be 'national in outlook', not provincial in that it slavishly followed the example of England, though perhaps parochial in the best sense that it would care for the parish of Wales, as Raymond Garlick once put it in a letter to me, but also truly 'international in outlook', not spuriously so, in that, rooted in Wales, it could look out confidently from time to time at what was happening elsewhere and show an awareness of the wider world. I made a start by commissioning reviews of new anthologies of Scottish poetry, one of which was by Edwin Morgan, now Poet Laureate of Scotland, and of books by Sorley Maclean, Octavio Paz, Theodore Roethke, Pablo Neruda, Robert Lowell, Michael Hamburger, George Seferis, Tristan Corbière and George Mackay Brown, as well as an article on modern Breton poetry. I also brought out special numbers devoted to a single poet – R.S. Thomas (Spring 1972), David Jones (Winter 1972) and Dafydd ap Gwilym (Spring 1973) – an innovation that has continued to the present day.

As for the charge that my magazine was a Nationalist publication, I must admit to being a bit bothered by it. Certainly it was born out of the editor's belief that English is one of the languages of Wales and the English-speaking Welsh have a vital part to play in the country's cultural life, and yes, I was an active member of Plaid Cymru at the time, as were some of my supporters and contributors; I'm still a member, as a matter of fact, though not so active these days. But there was nothing party political about it and, although I sometimes expressed 'Nationalist' sentiments, my editorials (except once when Alun Talfan Davies QC, who owned the magazine after 1967, demanded I rephrase a sentence to avoid upsetting the Gorsedd of Bards), I never let ideological considerations sway my literary judgement.

Of the 56 contributors to the first seven numbers, I think (though I can't be certain) about twenty were members or supporters of Plaid Cymru, including all ten of the Welsh-language writers. Harri Webb, Raymond Garlick, Tom Earley, Cyril Hodges, Anthony Conran, Colin Palfrey, Sally Roberts Jones, Peter Gruffydd, R.S. Thomas and Emyr Humphreys wore their party allegiance on their sleeve, and so there's little doubt about them. But others, like Dannie

Abse, John Ormond, Robert Morgan and John Stuart Williams, were almost certainly supporters, or even members, of the Labour Party. I'm not so sure about the political views of Vernon Watkins, Leslie Norris, Herbert Williams and Roland Mathias, and as for the rantipole John Tripp, I don't think he'd have been comfortable in any party except the boozy kind.

Even so, I was glad when in 1967 a phalanx of Nationalists and Socialists, including many of those already mentioned, supported my application to the Arts Council and when Gwyn Jones and T.J. Morgan, both Labour men and Chairman of the Welsh Committee and Literature Panel respectively, appointed me to the Literature Director's post.

Not that any of this was relevant to my role as editor of *PW.* I was as pleased to receive Dannie's 'In Llandough Hospital' or Leslie's 'Snow' or John Ormond's 'Cathedral Builders' as I was to get Herbert Williams's 'The Old Tongue' or Harri Webb's 'The Stone Face'. What I was after were good poems, regardless of the poets' politics; after all, my title was *Poetry Wales*, in that order.

My main drive was to bring out a magazine in which the English-language poets of Wales, and their readers, could see their work in a Welsh context. I was, from the start, keeping a weather eye out for new talents: many made their début in *PW* and the Autumn 1972 number was filled by poets, 34 in all, including Tony Curtis, Nigel Jenkins and Robert Minhinnick, who were appearing in the magazine, and in some cases in print, for the first time.

Just as heartening was to find older poets such as Glyn Jones, John Ormond, Leslie Norris, Raymond Garlick and Roland Mathias sending me new poems, encouraged by the fact that a magazine now existed specifically for the publication of their work.

Richard Gwyn
Letter from Greece

IT HAS BECOME a commonplace to grieve the horrors that tourism has unleashed in some of the most beautiful corners of the planet, even while reading *The Guardian* weekend travel section which bemoans the despoiling of yet another idyllic location at the same time as contributing to it. You know the line: the last unspoilt beach in X; the gorgeous mountain hike in Y when you can spend all day without seeing another living soul except some cheerful peasant with a donkey. The message is unequivocal: get there quick before more people like you get there, or worse, people unlike you, the cheaper operators, what the Greeks call 'Neckermanners' after the German tour company. Over the course of my childhood and early adulthood I saw parts of Greece transformed from destinations of idiosyncratic charm and genuine human warmth to embittered, cash-driven, xenophobic and cynical funhouses where Pudding Island's shaven headed stormtroopers and shrieking harpies swig beer, vomit, and foul-mouth the universe.

Still, I knew this was happening to Greece – in fact that was why I left, definitively in the mid 1980's. So why have I come back?

I had recently begun writing a novel, which was set during the cold war, and in which I needed a place where there was a sizeable American military base. I spent time in 1983 at the Comiso peace camp in Sicily – a kind of Italian Greenham Common – but Sicily didn't have the ambience I wanted, and in any case I did not know the Sicilians in the way I felt I knew the Greeks. Hania, the largest town in western Crete, is only a few kilometres from the large US naval base at Souda, so seemed the obvious choice. Besides, I had first hand experience of US naval ratings from working as a waiter in the famously insalubrious and atmospheric restaurant on Hania's Skridlov Street, once owned by Michaelis Kokkinakis, and now a tourist gift shop run by his son.

During 1981-2, it was my winter job, while in the summer I spent my time fishing on a wooden boat I had bought with the proceeds from an industrial accident, and generally hanging out.

Returning to Hania reminded me how fiction becomes established though a combination of retrospective and projected fantasy, along with the raw guts of memory superimposed on a real location. The writing of fiction is unique in this respect. It aims, ideally – and this is of course a personal and subjective view – to provide something (some would call it a truth) that is more exacting and vivid than that which lived experience usually provides, and yet uses our shared knowledge of lived experience in order to re-present that something. In this respect the writing of fiction differs from poetry. A part of poetry's unique attraction lies in its flexibility within a given form to say a certain amount within a short space, and to do so without necessarily covering a wide spectrum of lived experience in quite the same way. Poetry is a transformative process, a type of alchemy. The best poems tap directly into the unconscious, dragging out debris and sand and mud and rock fragments along with cracked water-jugs, broken umbrellas, stuffed animals and hydra-headed monsters. We never know what a good poem will deliver to our eyes (or our writing fingers); poetry relies on the twin processes of deep metaphor and sudden epiphany cocooned in sound. Fiction has a different task, though one which is not entirely at odds with that of poetry: perhaps the two are complementary, and that might be why I like to write both.

There is also another dimension to the writing of fiction: to what extent should the literary text map onto an extant or visible geography? If I want the location to have some kind of resonance for the reader it needs to be evoked with the maximum eye to small detail and yet without overburdening the narrative with a sense of place that is limited to a particular point in time, such as, in this instance, the Hania of 1981. Even if readers have never been to the places one inhabits in fiction, they can at least come away with a strong impression of what that place is like for them. Dickens' London, Proust's Paris, and Borges' Buenos Aires have all produced an atmospheric condition for a place (and a time) which I have not experienced and yet which feels intimately familiar to me now. Hania, of course, is not an international metropolis on the grand scale, but small as it is, it has served as a meeting place between three continents for many centuries, perched between Europe, Asia and Africa. This geographical fortuity has also rendered it a base for world powers over the years, hence its importance to the United States during the cold war and beyond.

There is always a sense of trepidation in returning to a place you have loved and lived in. True to my worst suspicions, the town and its environs had changed almost beyond recognition. The scale of consumerism, the heightening of 'local colour' for marketable effect – one in which traditional culture becomes a parody of itself – the appearance of estate agencies flogging holiday homes at outrageous prices, the substitution of *souvlaki* stands for fast food outlets, a brand new Virgin store on the main drag; all pointed to a familiar story. I spent the first morning shell-shocked in a hotel overlooking the Venetian harbour. It was too expensive, but it was my wife's birthday, and a bit of luxury counts on these occasions, especially following a 5.00 a.m. arrival after our ferry was stranded at Piraeus for two days due to bad weather.

Eventually I found the courage to walk down to the Splanzia, the old 'Turkish' quarter where I used to live. Gerasimou Street is almost entirely in ruins. Old Nikos' shop is no longer a shop. He must have died long ago – he was in his 70's in 1981. That shop served the little community of locals, gypsies and the prostitutes who lived across the way from us in a warren of red-light houses. But today I see no one I recognise. There are Albanians living in one of the few remaining habitable buildings. Graffiti has appeared on the walls in the little square at the bottom of the street. An anarchist icon and a black scrawl: XENOI ERGATES ADERFIA MAS – foreign workers are our brothers. No doubt this graffito signals the presence of a nationalist back-lash against the influx of Albanians and other eastern European itinerant labour. Years ago, there was a row of tin shacks where the gypsies lived. Friendly, effusive, less philo-sophical than the Greeks, they worked the fishing boats and sat about mending nets and drinking in the evenings. In those days, the little square with its small plane tree marked a sort of frontier between the territory of the brothels and Gerasimou, where I, a refugee from Thatcherism, lived with an Argentinian refugee from Videla's junta and a dog called Tango. Of course the Falklands war happened while we were here and it caused some amusement to the Greeks that the two of us should be such close friends. There were others, notably the more moronic British debris in the bars, who found it less amusing. Fortunately Cacho, my friend, was able to look after himself better than most.

Away from the ruins of my past life, Hania has become another victim of the contemporary obsession with wrecking the world. As though all the once special secret places have to be trammelled into a barbarous uniformity in order to make them saleable to the hordes who bring in currency and despair. The Cretans, who saw off serial invasions over cen-turies and sent the Turks and Germans packing during the space of sixty years in the last one, now seem intent on des-ecrating their own island.

From Hania we took a trip westward through the villages I used to visit half a lifetime ago. Maleme, Platanias, Gerani, Tavronitis: they have become absorbed into one unending strip of garish nightclubs, eateries, hideous hotels. They used to be discrete, identifiable places with individual character, living off the orange harvest, other small scale farming and fishing, with only a handful of tiny pensions between them. We drove twenty kilometres without a break through the bur-geoning of reinforced concrete before I finally accepted that there was no point in raging against this bleak metamorpho-sis. I headed inland with my family, over the White Mountains to a village in the south-west of the island, where difficulty of access and an unexcavated Minoan/Hellenic city has held the deluge at bay for at least a few more years.

The village is pleasant and hospitable and we spend Easter here, taking walks along the coastal cliffs in both directions and up to the mountains overlooking the plain of Omalos. One day we navigate the Ireni gorge, a less well-known though equally beautiful alternative to Samaria. On the last day in the village I take a dawn walk down to the small harbour as the sun rises over the outcrops of rock in a perfectly motionless sea. On my return, a large Greek stands at the side of the road undoing his fly, about to urinate. He notices me as I come alongside him. He pretends to be pre-occupied with his mobile phone rather than greet me. Perhaps he is embarrassed, a condition from which I believed the Greek male to be genetically immune. In the past, I think, a Greek would always have greeted you on the open road. Now they talk into mobile phones, whether or not there is anyone at the other end, just like people everywhere.

On the last evening my wife is laid low with gastric flu and I eat with my two young daughters at the Paterakis family restaurant. It is a mysterious evening, the awning flapping in a sudden wind straight from the Libyan desert. I happen to know that the Paterakis clan, from the next village of Koustogerako, was famous in these parts for producing some of the fiercest and most renowned of the guerrilla fighters resisting the Nazi occupation. In 1943, when the Germans scourged the villages of Moni, Levada and Koustogerako, they herded the women and children of this last village outside the church and lined them up in front of a machine gun. The men had climbed the rocks above the village and it was Costi Paterakis, who with a single shot, fired from 400 metres and killed the machine-gunner before he could open fire, causing the rout of the occupying troops. Sixty years on, in a grandson's restaurant, a large party of Germans is enjoying a meal at a neighbouring table. All is well in our united Europe. Then, without warning, two little blond boys leap onto the restaurant terrace with stick-guns, making rat-tat-tat machine gun sounds under the awning. Their father, visibly agitated, orders them in hushed tones to return to their play on the beach. I feel ambivalently about this. The father, had he known the particular significance of the family name under whose hospitality he was eating, would no doubt have been doubly humiliated. But can I not sympathise a little with the hindering turmoil such an inheritance brings with it? Here is a man of my age, with no responsibility for the war, feeling guilt for his sons (who have less than no responsibility) playing guns (which kids do everywhere). But evidently for blond German boys to play games of a certain kind in parts of Europe still conveys a deep sense of impropriety.

After returning to our room I read 'Late into the Night', the last poems of Yannis Ritsos. Ritsos has long been high on my list of favourite poets, and I started reading him here in Crete, so it is fitting to be doing so now. I remember him speaking at the huge KKE (Communist Party of Greece) rallies, and of his friend Theodorakis playing in Hania with the amazing Maria Farandouri. Theodorakis is mainly known to the rest of the world as the composer of the soundtracks for 'Zorba the Greek' and 'Z', but he has had a passionate involvement with politics throughout this life, like Ritsos enduring periods of imprisonment and exile. The day after one particular concert I had to fly to Athens and arriving on the plane the great man with his shaggy curls and fierce eyebrows looked up from his papers in the first class section and greeted me with a surprising smile, no doubt mistaking me for someone I was not. I mumbled something back at him and asked myself whether famous communists really ought to travel first class, and what the party line was on this subject. Theodorakis also held strong views on the despoiling of Greece by tourism and it was around this time that he was charged with attacking (actually firing at) some Swedish nude bathers on the beach below his house. Ritsos in turn regarded the disintegration of rural Greek life as symptomatic both of the destruction of a symbolic landscape as well as the triumph of global capitalism at the expense of his beloved communism. He saw this dual catastrophe occurring in the last years of his life, leaving a haunted and despairing poetry in his wake. As usual he worked on three or four collections at a time; one in first draft form, one or two in states of revision, and another undergoing final editing. In one of these last poems, entitled 'Useless Keys', he writes:

> This far and no farther. There is no farther.
> The local bus unloads foreign tourists,
> foreign luggage, foreign sleeping bags.
> You don't even recognize the suitcase
> that once held something of yours –
> a favourite blue shirt, that snapshot
> of your first love. The books on the shelves
> turn their backs, the heap of keys
> on the table – you don't know
> and don't care what locks they fit…

A sense of inconsolable loss accompanies many of these poems. Yet, as he readies himself for death, he finds a sort of ruminative solace in being "hypnotized by sunlight between two unknowable miracles" and the poems carry both the candour and sadness of one who recognises that his lifelong aspirations will never be fulfilled, that in the end it matters not at all what locks might fit the useless keys. After this trip, I share his sadness, and at least one aspect of his nostalgia.

Zoë Brigley
Lizard

A pre-clinical dopaminergic deficit precedes clinically evident Parkinson's Disease by many years. An event or process that ultimately results in disease may occur or begin in youth.

Sixty years ago paddling on the Gulf:
the tar of black gold, mahogany docked
at port, its sap rich with schemes of money.

The girl on the pier points a long finger
from the flat Caye to the Caribbean.
Ashore, her house with the green porch.

A woman sings in Spanish in a house
further down; the father on the veranda
puts his pince-nez to his nose to look out to sea.

Leaves poke out from the centre of palms
like so many hands on the face of a clock.
I trail my boots in the dust, she in bare feet.

Later she traces an eye in the sand: sketch
of a window, mock of an Indian tattoo.
A broom leans at the corner of the house.

I run down the long pier in the dark and leap
—underwater blood moves in circles about my ears,
the seething coral, membranous as brains or red as coals.

I pull on a wet boot but something squirms to life,
a small green lizard emerges to streak the sand
and climb the side of the clapboard house

and to bend again over that sodden boot
is to feel the fine flexing of my spine,
to sense the heavy weight about my shoulders,
to taste the beetle that sits on my tongue.

Other anthologies from Seren...

TWENTIETH CENTURY ANGLO-WELSH POETRY
Edited by Dannie Abse

Wales was the source of some of the finest poetry of the last century, from the modernism of David Jones through the powerful lyrics of Dylan Thomas and the understatement of R.S. Thomas to a host of talented younger poets. In this, the definitive anthology of 'Anglo-Welsh' poetry, Dannie Abse, himself an important poet, has chosen the outstanding poets and poems of the period, displaying a breadth and variety which belies the notion of 'regional poetry'. First published in 1997, this new edition brings the century completely up to date with the inclusion of work by outstanding new poets Owen Sheers, Sarah Corbett, Frances Williams and Samantha Wynne-Rhydderch.

1-85411-356-9 | £9.99 | 279pp
www.seren-books.com

WELSH VERSE
Fourteen centuries of poetry
Translations by Tony Conran

The traditions of Welsh poetry stretch back
to the sixth century, making it one of the
oldest living literatures in Europe. In *Welsh Verse*,
(formerly *The Penguin Book of Welsh Verse*),
Tony Conran translates a selection from
fourteen centuries of poetry, from the epics
of Taliesin and Aneirin to modern poets such as
Gwyn Thomas and Nesta Wyn Jones. En route
he takes in sagas and carols, hymns and strict
metres, Romantics and Social Realists. The poetic
movements of Welsh-language verse are charted
in Conran's influential Introduction, in which he
explains the important role of poetry in Welsh
history.

1-85411-081-0 | £9.95 | 355pp
www.seren-books.com

POETRY WALES:
25 Years
Edited by Cary Archard

Fifteen years before the current anthology, *Poetry Wales* took its first retrospective look at its own achievements. This selection of 117 contributions is a fascinating record of *Poetry Wales*' first 25 years. It includes not only poetry but also articles about poets such as Dylan Thomas and Gwenallt, and controversial letters and editorials on Anglo-Welsh poetry and politics.

Poetry Wales has always embraced the wide world of poetry outside Wales. Although this anthology focuses on Welsh writers, the magazine's range is represented by poets such as Herbert and Heaney and by articles as diverse as 'Women's Poetry' and 'Poetry in the USA'.

1-85411-031-4 | £6.99 | 257pp
www.seren-books.com